Race versus Robe:
The Dilemma of Black Judges

by

Michael David Smith

National University Publications
ASSOCIATED FACULTY PRESS, INC.
Port Washington, New York • 1983

Manufactured in the United States of America

Published by
Associated Faculty Press, Inc.
Port Washington, N.Y.

Library of Congress Cataloging in Publication Data

Smith, Michael David,
    Race versus robe.

    (National university publications)
    Bibliography: p.
    Includes index.
    1. Afro-American judges.   I. Title.
KF8775.S63   1983   347.73′14′08996073   83-7053
ISBN O-8046-9320-X   347.3071408996073

Dedicated

with love

to

Madie Roberts Smith
my mother

and

Sarah Thompson Moore
my paternal great-aunt

and

to the memory

of

Mary Thompson Smith
my paternal grandmother

and

Irene Smith
my cousin

Contents

Acknowledgments

The *auteur* theory has gained widespread acceptance in recent years among film fans. While it has commendably redressed the neglect of the director in the movie-making process, it has probably gone to an extreme and overlooked other significant contributors to the quality of the product. This theory is based on the assumption that the author is the creator of his book. But ironically, the author, at least of a nonfiction work, is usually indebted to a host of individuals and institutions.

Financial debts, often the most persistent kind, are relatively easy to recognize in my case. The Ford Foundation and the College of Wooster (Ohio) kindly provided funds to research and type this project.

Debts to the judges, friends, and professors who were instrumental in the preparation of this book are difficult to repay. The problem flows from two sources: the ineffectiveness of words and my faulty memory. Though English is a rich language, words of thanks can merely hint at my gratitude to all who contributed to this product. Moreover, my memory bank has failed me—I have forgotten the names of some contributors. Yet I will always remember their spirit of encouragement and aid.

The names of those who made substantial donations come readily to mind and merit special mention: the black judges who responded to my questionnaire and, even more, those eleven who granted personal interviews; my brother Kenneth Roberts Smith; the Hammonds of Baltimore—"Chuck," Leslie, and O'Neill; typists Priscilla Savoy (Baltimore), Donna Massaro (Wooster), and Gina Nadas (New Orleans); editors Marilyn Silverman and Evelyn Martin; at the College of Wooster, Professors Bradlee Karan, Yvonne Williams, and Frank Miller and his wife Martha; and at Johns Hopkins University, Professors Milton Cummings, Steven Stephens, Robert Peabody, and especially J. Woodford Howard.

Once, when President Harry Truman was particularly irked over a harsh review of his daughter's singing recital, he called the reviewer a SOB. A wag of a radio commentator translated the phrase for his listeners as Servant of the Brotherhood. To all contributors to this book, named and unnamed, I salute you as SOBs—Servants of the Brotherhood. I hope the quality of this publication matches the generous spirit of your contributions to it.

September 5, 1981   Michael David Smith
New Orleans

Chapter 1
Introduction

The law is a political instrument—and black Americans are of a divided mind. Such is the myth and ignorance that surrounds law and race in the United States that both of these statements may startle many observers. Both phrases also may seem incongruent in their juxtaposition.

The law is a political instrument because it is intimately tied into government. Making and enforcing rules are among the primary duties of any government. The imposition of rules authoritatively allocates values. The dominant interests in a society use their power to prescribe certain forms of conduct and exploit impotent groups. The relationship between the dominant and subjugated groups operates from many different perspectives, with class, sex, and race being among them. The law as legislated, interpreted, and enforced, merely reflects these realities. When United States Chief Justice Roger T. Taney, in the infamous *Dred Scott* decision, stated that "the black man had no rights which the white man was bound to respect," he was merely articulating the prevalent thought of the white Americans of his time.

The Taney example illustrates two points. The first is the use of the law as a political tool to reenforce the subjugated position of black Americans, the law merely reflecting the will of the dominant group in society. The second point illustrates the power of the judge. In their *Dred Scott* decision, Taney and his brethren invalidated a thirty-five-year-old congressional statute and hastened the advent of the American Civil War. As courts are political institutions, so judges are politicians empowered by the state to determine who gets what, when, and how. Judges resolve conflicts—conflicts involving life, liberty, money, office, and reputation. In the courtroom aggrieved parties invoke governmental powers in order to impose their claims upon other parties. In interpreting the law and deciding which claims have merit, judges impute values, including their own, into their decisions.

For a long time, black Americans were presumptively among the losers before American law. That legal status is evinced by Taney's comment. At the founding

1

of the Republic, blacks were assessed for tax and representational purposes as three fifths of a person in the Constitution, the basic law of the law. Even after they were emancipated from slavery, their status was still unequal before the law. And it was not until the 1950s that black Americans finally began to achieve greater legal rights, most notably in the *Brown* decision in which the Supreme Court declared school segregation unconstitutional.

The fruits of the fight for black equity before the law came most spectacularly in the 1960s. Long considered outsiders, Afro-Americans began to win the political power that is always reflected in the administration of the law. Numerous blacks captured official positions at all levels of government. By 1981, there were over 5,000 blacks holding such positions.

Judgeships are among the public offices to which Afro-Americans have recently attained. Given the pervasive racism of American society, blacks have very rarely occupied any position in the legal enforcement system. But the black judge has been especially rare. When Robert Morris was appointed to Boston's Magistrates Court in 1852, he became the first Afro-American to hold an American judicial position. For a century after his appointment, less than two dozen blacks held judgeships. Black exclusion from the judiciary has abated somewhat in the last quarter-century, and black judges have increased most rapidly since the mid-1960s. There are now over 500 judicial posts held by Afro-Americans. Positioned at every level from justice of the peace to associate justice of the United States Supreme Court, most are on state trial benches.

Since courts were instrumental in legitimizing the inequality of black Americans, the black judge is in an ironic position. While overt legalized racism is disappearing, there remains covert institutionalized racism. This latter form of race discrimination is more subtle and more pervasive because it is predicated upon nonracial factors such as class and culture. Since almost all questions in the United States are eventually resolved into judicial ones, the black judge is in a position to recognize and help remedy both forms of racism.

But in doing his job, the black judge will be torn by the two different urges that threaten to rend most black Americans. While these urges are not necessarily contradictory, they are quite often incompatible in practice. They could be divided, somewhat simplistically, along poles of racial separation and integration. This schism within the self of individual black Americans has been noted as early as W.E.B. DuBois' observation that

> One ever feels his twoness—an American, a Negro; two souls, two thoughts, two unreconciled strivings; two warring ideals in one dark body, whose dogged strength alone keeps it from being torn asunder.

But the division within each black person is without doubt much older than this eloquently phrased comment. The question itself must be as old as the first African slave to land on the shores of what became known as America.

The poles of racial separation and integration have many variations and gradations. Separation can mean something as grandiose if improbable as a separate, sovereign political state. This was the ultimate objective of Marcus Garvey. But separation can also denote the wish to live among blacks. This was one of the more benign aspects of the philosophy of Booker T. Washington. Sharing a common group identity and purpose is probably the mildest form of separation, since it implicitly allows for the physical integration of the races. This was at times the hope of DuBois and for a long time the faith of the National Association for the Advancement of Colored People (NAACP).

The fact that these individuals are judges in the American political system indicates that they are not separatists, at least not doctrinaire ones. But such are the irradiations of the duality that confounds black Americans that even integrationist judges will be caught in the crossfire of remaining loyal to their race or obeisant to the dictates of their robe. There are sound arguments for each choice, but there are also unpleasant consequences.

Almost four centuries of discrimination by European-Americans has had a profound influence on Afro-Americans: It helped to foster a strong group identity so as to buffer the slights and stigmas imposed by whites. Racism has driven blacks to anxiety, anger, and activity. These judges are the products, directly or indirectly, of the activity of black political groups. If this obligation was not enough by itself, it is reenforced by the daily examples of recurring race bigotry. Finally, the failure to keep faith with their black constituents will subject the judges to the opprobrium of members of their own race. Radical blacks will accuse them of being traitors to their race and of consorting with the enemy. They will very likely be ostracized by their own people. While the ostracism may not be known and reported in the popular media, the slurs of black judges in their clubs, churches, and even in their families, may nevertheless be disconcerting.

The robe of the judge has traditionally symbolized impartiality on the bench and the eschewing of partisan activities off it. The judicial role is a very circumscribed one: the judge must avoid even the appearance of favoritism and he is expected to shun all controversial issues. Indeed, the demands of the robe are so strict that over nine tenths of the judges in Florida felt it inappropriate for judicial incumbents to take stands on issues. While over eight tenths of these judges declared it improper to criticize an opponent's conduct or even his qualifications for judicial office, less than half thought it fitting for judges to speak at political rallies. However, given the long-noted tendency of American political questions to become legal ones and the increasing litigiousness of Americans, there are compelling reasons for judges to remain above the raging frays. But if, driven by his own race concerns, the black judge assumes a racially activist position on the bench, he faces the sanctions of the bench and obloquy from his community. From the bench, bar, police, and the media, will likely come demands for his reassignment, recall, or even impeachment.

The demands of his race and the dictates of his robe are the dual dilemmas facing the black judge. One black judge asserted boldly that his duty is to "shake up" the status quo, while another whispered that "every black who is a judge walks on eggshells. You learn that lesson early or you don't survive." How have black judges in their own minds decided the issues of race versus robe? This is the subject of our examination.

There haven't been many studies of black judges because they are so recent an addition to American politics. Our study draws a collective portrait of Afro-American judges throughout the country as of 1973. The first part focuses on their socioeconomic background; on the sources and periods of interest and activity in law, politics, and civil rights; on career patterns; on recruitment to the judiciary; and on their perceptions of the judicial role. The second part correlates selected background factors with role perceptions. This examination will then allow us to discuss the influences that shape the attitudes of black judges, to speculate on their impact on the American judiciary, and to assess the analytical value of role theory.

Throughout this study, the influence of race on Afro-American jurists is one of the threads to be unraveled. Jewish and Catholic religions are considered minority faiths in the United States and have been treated as influential factors on judicial decision-making. Black is today almost synonymous with the word *minority*. Yet any one attribute, racial or religious, must vie with many other influences on the lives of individuals. In addition, the impact of a particular trait will vary from one individual to another. While we expect race to be an important influence on the attitudes of black judges, the impact may be tempered by other factors, especially the judicial role. Our examination will help us gauge the interplay of race, professionalism, and other attributes, on the role perceptions of our subjects. Since role provide the backdrop for this study, a discussion of its elements is required.

Few recent concepts in the social sciences have been as widely used as role theory. Though enjoying great popularity over the past quarter-century, it is a very murky research tool. There seem to be as many definitions of its terms as there are social scientists to state them. For clarification, it may be best to approach role theory as a series of distinctions: (1) position and role; (2) role consensus and role conflict; (3) expectations and sanctions; and (4) role conflict among actors and role competition within an actor.

The distinction between positions and roles is often misunderstood. Position refers to a unit of a social structure, a point in a system of recurring relationships. But a role is a unit of culture; it refers to the rights and duties, the normatively approved patterns of behavior expected of the occupants of a given position.

Moreover, the process of defining roles is a dynamic one. It is a culmination of the interaction of two or more position occupants in a group structure. After the group is initially established, there is confusion among the actors over the duties of their respective positions. As members of the group interact, they develop shared expectations, which are the norms specifying the appropriate behavior for each position occupant.

The agreement on expectations is called role consensus. The enforcement of these norms is achieved through the use of sanctions, positive and negative, which may be applied by role partners (external) or by the actor himself (internal). Role consensus is also maintained through the socialization of new group members in behavior and values.

Yet, even given the methods for maintaining consensus, there is always the potential for role conflict. Disagreement among role partners may appear along social, cultural, and personal dimensions. Socially, the actor and his role partners may disagree about (1) the expectations included in a given role; (2) the range of permitted or prohibited behavior; (3) whether the expected behavior is mandatory or simply preferred; (4) situations in which roles apply; and (5) which expectations will be honored first. Moreover, since norms reflect values, role consensus may founder on cultural differences among group members. A system of beliefs or ideology based on different cultural values may provoke conflict among the actor and his fellow group members. Disagreements are especially likely if one of the actors is a member of a newly powerful subculture. Finally, most roles allow the personality of each position occupant to shape the interaction among members of a group structure. Personality is thus a source of role conflict. An actor may lack certain abilities and attributes necessary for the successful enactment of the role others expect of him. In addition, he may have self-concepts, attitudes, and personality needs contrary to the expectations of his role partners. When conflicts arise, group members are provoked into clarifying their roles. Consensus is sought by formalizing relations between role partners in specific terms, ensuring standard socialization, and developing ceremonies to increase each partner's identification with the group's goals. Frequently, such consensus-building mechanisms fail, especially where expectations governing relations have sharply different policy implications for each participant and where the disadvantaged role partner has recently gained greater power.

While role conflict often involves disagreements between role partners, there is another form of tension that focuses exclusively on the individual actor. When a person occupying one role is subjected, either by others or by himself, to incompatible expectations, he suffers from role competition. The actor will not be able to honor both expectations because of limitations of time and energy or because of opposing psychological sets. As there are mechanisms for building consensus between role partners, there are also comparable ones for role competition within the individual. The pressured actor will most likely honor the role expectations held by the reference group that is most compatible with his own self-concept.

For all its imprecise terminology, role theory is useful for ordering social interaction. For example, one black judge in New York City followed a low-bail policy during his infrequent assignments to arraignment court. Indicting jails as "nigger and Hispanic zoos, with mostly white keepers," he assessed low bails to enable defendants to secure pretrial release and, because of their financial stake, to guarantee their appearance at trial. But the police association was so infuriated by this practice, especially when defendants were accused of assaulting policemen, that it publicly clamored for the judge's removal. Before he was transferred from criminal to civil court, however, the lengthy dispute had become so controversial that a group of citizens picketed in support of the judge and his policy. Later, attorneys in the Legal Aid Society criticized the transfer and questioned the role of the police in the administration of the courts.

Though the judge was eventually reassigned to the criminal court after a three-year stint on the civil bench, this dispute illustrates the utility of role theory by evoking most of its major elements. Role consensus is implied in the conflict between the police and this particular judge. The police expected him to act in the same manner as other judges in that jurisdiction, especially in cases of alleged attacks on policemen. The criticisms by the police and the transfer of the judge point out the use of sanctions to enforce role expectations. Furthermore, this conflict over roles was so intense because it involved a disagreement over values. The judge and his supporters favored a due process model of criminal justice, which emphasizes the innocence of the accused until proven guilty in court and decries the notion that the quality of a defendant's trial should depend on the amount of money he has. The police and their allies, on the other hand, advocated a crime control model, which stresses speed and efficiency in repressing criminal behavior. Just as role theory has applications to social interaction, this argument over values has implications for social policy. For instance, one study of New York City found that defendants detained before trial were almost twice as likely to be convicted as those who were able to make bail.

This example of conflict between judge and police underscores the relevance of our study of the competing factors that shape the role attitudes of the black bench. However, the problem of role conflict challenging the black bench is not peculiar to the judiciary. It is a predicament that faces every black who moves into a formerly white-dominated situation. Each will be perplexed over whether to follow the traditional path, with all its connotations of racial oppression, or to chart a new course, based upon his experiences. Moreover, the twoness of black Americans are not distinctively confined to professions, but may be witnessed on a purely personal level as well. Three examples suffice to illustrate the duality that confounds Afro-Americans and also point out the widespread ramifications of our study of the black judiciary.

Just as blacks have begun to move onto the American bench, they have moved into other positions in the legal system, for instance, as prison guards and police officers. Jacobs and Kraft, comparing young black prison guards with white rural ones, conclude that while some attitudinal differences were found toward prisoners, correctional goals, administrators, and the role of the guard, these variances were not consistent enough to conclude that blacks will perform their job differently than whites. Yet a federal jury in New Orleans awarded $73,000 in

June 1981 to a former member of that city's police force. The young black had been fired from the department after he refused to sign a report covering for the "excessive" use of force by his partner, also black. His refusal contravened an unwritten, traditional code of police agencies. Thus, he was charting a new course while his partner was maintaining the traditional one.

And finally, though traditional role studies have focused on formal organizations, there are informal situations in which role and race can be illuminated. In May 1980, one black community in Miami erupted in rage over the acquittal of the local police in the unprovoked murder of a black executive. Though three whites were killed in the ensuing riot, only one black person persevered in her testimony against the group of blacks accused of the murders. For her effort, she was ostracized by her community. Still, this woman's sense of justice prevailed over her allegiance to her group. In her "betrayal," we can detect the importance of race in American society, and observe the use of sanctions to maintain role expectations, even in informal settings.

The influence of race has been viewed as the most prominent feature in the makeup of blacks. One observer has asserted that Afro-Americans are the only people in the American system who, as a group, desire change. An eminent black jurist has commented that "a black judge, by nature, in this historical period, has got to be a reformist. . . The whole purpose for selecting him is that the people are dissatisfied with the status quo. . . His role is to shake it up." A black judge's exercise of power is not going to necessarily be the same as that of a white judge, he continues, because "a judge is a product of his experiences." The focus of this study is on the influence of these experiences, most especially racial and professional ones, on the black judge and on his perception of his judicial duties.

Afro-Americans as a group have always occupied an unequal position in this country, and this inequality continues today economically, politically, and socially. While judges are powerful, they are usually confined to microscopic remedies for each case as it is brought to them by the disputants. The use of the power of judges may be shaped not only by the facts of the particular cases before them, but by how each case fits into a larger situation.

In deciding the question of whether to cling to race or flee to the judicial role as the touchstone of the exercise of his powers, the black judge sees a different world than the one in which he grew to adulthood. He sees many signs that whites are now willing to accept blacks as equal partners in the American polity. But he also sees equal, if not greater, evidence that blacks are still being subjugated.

The results of public opinion polls provide both hope and dismay. While only two fifths of whites surveyed in 1958 said that they would vote for a black presidential candidate, four fifths said as much two decades later. But even though over half of the whites thought in 1981 that blacks were better off than they were ten years ago, less than a fifth of the blacks responded in a like fashion. And in the period from 1956 to 1980, the number of whites who favored school integration, increased from half to almost nine tenths. However, almost half of the white parents who would not object to sending their children to a school with only a few black students did object to sending them to a school whose enrollment was more than half black. Given the pervasiveness of residential segregation by race throughout the nation, many observers maintain that school integration can only be achieved at least in the short run through busing. But in 1980, less than a fifth of the whites favored busing to achieve racial balance in the schools, though two thirds of the blacks approved it.

If the United States is to realize any significant racial mingling, blacks must have the opportunity to choose where they wish to live. And there has been an increase in the percentages of whites who believe that blacks should have the right to live anywhere they can afford. In 1968, less than two thirds indicated as much, but over nine tenths thought so ten years later. Yet over half of the whites canvassed in 1981 in a separate survey said that a homeowner should be able to decide for himself whether to sell his house to blacks; however three quarters of the blacks believed that the homeowner should not be able to refuse on racial grounds. The ability of blacks to afford housing raises economic issues. Blacks have faced discrimination for 350 years. Affirmative action programs have been instituted to ameliorate the distinctions between the races. However, almost three quarters of the whites declared that blacks who need help from the government should not receive it as long as white people in similar circumstances are not recipients of such aid.

In general, whites have an optimistic view of the progress made by blacks over the past quarter-century. For example, in 1981 almost two thirds were convinced that the police in most cities treated blacks as fairly as they treated whites. And only 6 percent believed that blacks were discriminated against in getting a quality education; 17 percent in getting decent housing; 13 percent in wages paid in most jobs; and 21 percent in getting skilled labor jobs. Each of the white responses, however, was significantly less than those of blacks.

Stereotypes may have been driven from popular, public conversation, but large numbers of whites still retain set images of blacks. For instance, half of the whites in 1978 agreed that blacks tend to have less ambition than whites; over a third believed that blacks want to live off handouts; somewhat less than a third maintained that blacks breed crime; a quarter stated that blacks have less native intelligence than whites; slightly less than a sixth asserted that blacks cared less for their family than whites; and a seventh responded that blacks are generally inferior to white people. These attitudes are all moderately to significantly less than the numbers uncovered fifteen years ago.

The ambivalent attitudes of whites on racial matters may find their counterpart in the disposition of black judges as they approach their bench duties. The wariness of whites toward blacks is likely to increase the anxiety of black judges in their choice of reference groups. However, the cited white attitudes may be seen as flimsy and circumstantial evidence in the equation confounding our respondents. Examples of white behavior may be seen as more determinative of the role perceptions of the Afro-American judiciary.

Though there are allegations that blacks are discriminated against in civil litigations, it is in the criminal sector of the legal process where racial inequities can be most clearly seen. Afro-Americans constitute a disproportionate number of police arrests. For example, though blacks composed only 20 percent of the population of New York City in 1973, they accounted for over 60 percent of all arrests. Indeed, they provided an almost equal percentage of persons killed by the police of that city. The report of 1973 shootings by New York police may appear to be a one-shot phenomenon, so to speak, the fluke of one year or of one jurisdiction. However, an examination of the shootings of the Los Angeles policy by Meyer indicates otherwise. Of 584 suspects shot at by the Los Angeles police from 1974 to 1978, whose race was known, considerably over half (55 percent) were blacks, though they comprised only a sixth of the general population of that sprawling California city. While 42 percent of all assaults on the police with a deadly weapon were committed by blacks, 55 percent of suspects shot at, 53 percent of those hit, and 50 percent of those shot fatally, were black. These findings do not appear to be a mishap, for over half of the suspects shot at in a three-and-a-half-year period from 1968 to 1971 were black. The pattern is repeated in 1979 in all aspects, except that 62 percent of those fatally shot by the police were black.

Hispanics and whites who constitute much larger percentages of the population of Los Angeles than blacks, were each involved in slightly over a fifth of such shooting incidents. In a curious twist, though a quarter of assaults with a deadly weapon against the police were committed by Hispanics, only 16 percent of those shot fatally were Hispanic.

These revelations continue like waves upon the shore, dashing one on top of the other. Though police would be more likely to shoot at blacks than Hispanics, or whites, following a refusal to halt and while appearing to reach for a weapon (27 percent versus 15 percent versus 18 percent), a greater proportion of blacks were ultimately determined to have been unarmed (28 percent versus 22 percent versus 20 percent). Though blacks were somewhat more likely to have guns than the other two groups, they were much less likely to have other weapons, such as knives.

Whenever the black community becomes enraged over police brutality involving the shooting of blacks, they are invariably counseled by due process advocates to allow the legal system the time to mete out justice. But Meyer's findings question the political and moral efficacy of this advice. A larger percentage of such shootings were found to be within police department policy or were less deserving of administrative disapproval than was the case when Hispanics or whites were so victimized. For example, administrative disapproval, which can range from a warning to actual termination, was imposed in a third of the cases where blacks were found to be unarmed when shot at, but was imposed in over two fifths of the cases involving Hispanics and almost half of the cases involving whites.

Yet this study of police shootings is only one aspect of the relationship between blacks and the criminal enforcement system. The heavy representation of blacks in criminal statistics continues in the more advanced steps of the criminal process. A plethora of research data signifies that Meyer's findings on police shootings in Los Angeles are not anomalous. What has been recently designated as institutional racism may be nothing more than a euphemism for whites to practice covert race discrimination. Economics, manners, and culture, the backbone of the argument for institutional racism, may serve to cover up personal race bias.

Though blacks comprise less than a eighth of the nation's population, they constituted more than a quarter of those arrested in 1978. Yet a 1974 study by Hepburn of almost thirty thousand adult arrests in a large midwestern city found that nonwhites had a larger proportion than whites of police arrests that were not upheld by the issuance of a warrant by the district attorney. This is so even when the offense, age, sex, and racial composition of the neighborhood were held constant. Though there were no significant differences in warrant refusals between the races for Part I offenses (such as homicide, rape, assault, burglary, and larceny over fifty dollars), there were racial disparities for Part II offenses (such as vagrancy, prostitution, gambling, and drunkenness). For example, for the latter category of offenses, warrants were refused by the district attorney for 57 percent of nonwhite males and 72 percent of nonwhite females, compared to 47 percent of white males and 54 percent of white females. Time, money, and insufficient evidence are all factors in the prosecutor's decision to refuse warrants, but the suspicion lingers that the police are abusing their discretionary powers and discriminating on the basis of race. Given the relative powerlessness of blacks and the relative invisibility of black neighborhoods to whites, it is perhaps not surprising to learn that police arrests of nonwhites, especially of males, in nonwhite enclaves are significantly more likely to have warrants refused than either white arrests in these same locations or nonwhite arrests outside them. Coupled with Meyer's finding that there were much greater percentages of blacks fatally shot by police in black neighborhoods than of major crimes committed there, this raises the harrowing prospect that black neighborhoods are subjected to two criminal elements—civilian and police. Furthermore, Hepburn's observations are all the more distressing when you consider that district attorneys in general have not traditionally been considered stalwart protectors of the rights of blacks.

After the arrest, arraignment and bail-setting are the next stages of the criminal process. Blacks fared no better here than at earlier steps. By the end of 1978, blacks constituted almost half of the inmates of local jails who were either denied bail or unable to raise it. Economics or class distinctions are used to explain the disproportionate numbers of blacks still in jail awaiting trial. Putting aside the fact that there are more than twice as many poor whites as there are poor blacks in absolute numbers, there are again signs that race is the major determinant of cases involving blacks. For example, one study of persons indicted for murder, rape, aggravated assault, and aggravated robbery, discovered that less than half of the whites were assessed bail of two thousand dollars or more, but over seven tenths of the blacks were. This research project was flawed because it failed to correlate race with criminal offense. After all, blacks could have been charged with more serious crimes than whites.

Yet Pope confined his attention to burglary arrestees during a one-year period across six California jurisdictions, and race was found to be a factor in the decision to release burglary suspects following arrest. In general, almost a quarter of the whites were released but less than a seventh of the blacks were. Less than a tenth of the blacks with no prior record were freed compared to almost a third of similarly situated whites. Even with no prior criminal record, blacks were still substantially more likely to be confined in jail than whites.

In general, the rule of penology is that the more severe the punishment, the more likely blacks are to be well represented. A study of defendants who pleaded guilty or who were convicted of violent crimes illustrates this point. Whites drew jail sentences in over two fifths of the cases, whereas blacks were sentenced almost two thirds of the time. Not only were Afro-Americans imprisoned more often than whites, but they also received longer sentences (seven months or longer for half of the whites but for over two thirds of the blacks). In addition, in the southern quadrant that runs from Alabama to Virginia, a 1978 study detected the same numbers of blacks and whites serving one- to five-year sentences, but substantially greater numbers of blacks than whites were serving longer than five years. Indeed, there were two to three times as many blacks sentenced to eleven or more years as whites.

The more frequent and lengthier terms of imprisonment for blacks is a widespread practice and partially explains why Afro-Americans constituted almost half (47 percent) of the nation's over 300,000 prisoners by the end of 1978. This figure has increased from 43 percent in 1970. The black three quarters of the Maryland prison population and the seven tenths of the Louisiana system are extreme but indicative of the racial composition of American penal institutions.

Blacks are disproportionately incarcerated in the United States for other reasons as well. Discretionary justice was examined by Poole and Regoli in a medium-security prison for adult male felons, and racism was also discerned in this closed system. While black and white rule-breaking was equally likely, blacks were more likely to be officially reported for infractions. The report, itself a product of race bias, influences subsequent sanctioning decisions, thus amplifying racism. Moreover, records of infractions help to determine prison assignments, and both in turn influence parole boards. The absurd circle continues, and black prisoners proliferate.

Nevertheless, true to the penological rule of thumb, racial disparities in sentencing are most noticeable in the ultimate sanction of the death penalty.

Though blacks provided approximately 10 percent of the nation's population between 1930 and 1966, they accounted for over half of the nation's executions. Of the almost 800 persons under sentence of death nationwide by April 1981, two fifths were black, with other minorities furnishing an additional 5 percent. Given this history, it is perhaps not surprising that in 1978 sixth tenths of all blacks surveyed opposed capital punishment, though seven tenths of the whites canvassed favored it.

Yet only half of the story of race and the death penalty has been told. After scrutinizing the four largest death-row states in the mid-1970s (Florida, Georgia, Texas, and Ohio), Bowers and Pierce have concluded that the race of the victim is the dispositive factor in the decision of whether to invoke the death penalty. For example, in Florida, a murderer (irrespective of race) who killed a white person was eleven times more likely to be sentenced to death than one who killed a black. The same relationship was true for Georgia. In Texas, however, the ratio was 22 to 1. In Ohio, merciful Ohio, the death penalty was only five times as likely to be returned for a white victim as for a black one, though the Buckeye State was most likely of the four to send all murderers to death row.

Shifting our angle slightly to examine interracial murders (blacks of whites and whites of blacks), we find the same pattern. For the four states combined, 17 percent of the blacks who killed whites were sentenced to death, but less than 1 percent of the whites who slayed blacks were similarly punished. Capital punishment studies demonstrate that, compared to whites, the lives of blacks are doubly discounted as victim and as murderer.

The death penalty is not often invoked in the United States compared to the numbers of murders. It is a capricious and arbitrary process, the American version of Russian roulette. However, in its freakish invocation, we catch flashes of racism run amok.

This broad sweep across the law enforcement system indicates the prevalence of race bias, yet this is the same evidence that confronts and confounds black judges as they discharge their duties. Though constituting less than 3 percent of the American judiciary, the Afro-American judge is made especially important by the lack of other blacks in powerful positions in the legal and political system. Though such information is not usually compiled, the police forces in major cities appear to remain overwhelmingly white, particularly in the upper echelons, even though the forces have increased black representation in the last decade. Yet the cities they patrol are heavily populated by blacks. By 1979, the Census Bureau estimated that 10 percent of the nation's police and detectives were black (which may include private police), and this is a 50-percent improvement over the figure of a decade earlier.

In selected cities, the disparities between the proportion of black police to black populations is even more pronounced, even with recent improvements. Blacks comprise over 55 percent of the population of New Orleans but provide only 21 percent of the police force, which is itself over three times more than the

1973 figure. Two fifths of Chicago is black but only one fifth of its police are, even though the department has been under a federal court order since 1977 to increase the minority proportion to 40 percent. Blacks make up 6 percent of the Los Angeles police, which is only a third of their percentage of the general population. And here again, a federal court has ordered an increase in the proportion of both blacks and Hispanics. Yet these figures on the numbers of blacks in police departments mask the racial composition of their commanders. By 1978, Greer reports that there were only 2 blacks for every 29 captains on the Newark force; only 32 blacks for every 268 lieutenants or above in the District of Columbia; and only 61 blacks for every 1,200 sergeants in Detroit. All of the three cities have had black mayors for one term or more.

But the token numbers of black police are greater than the percentage of black prosecutors, which is also difficult to discover. While the United States Department of Justice is 16 percent black in its total employment, only 4.3 percent of its attorneys are black. The attorney general of Louisiana has a force of staff attorneys that is a quarter black; this is apparently far greater than that of any other state. In 1970, the last reported date for a nationwide figure, only 2.3 percent of state and local prosecutors were Afro-Americans. This underrepresentation in the district attorney's office can be graphically illustrated. In 1974, there were only 58 blacks out of almost 1,600 prosecutors in twelve large cities where a quarter of America's black population resided.

The black legal pool from which judges, prosecutors, and defense counsels can be drawn, has historically been small, though there have been black lawyers since at least 1844. Their numbers have increased slightly since that time, with a quickened pace since 1970. By 1910, there were 800 Afro-American barristers; there was over a fivefold increase to 4,200 by 1970. However, ten years later, there were 12,000 black legal counsels. While the increase in absolute numbers may seem impressive, the growth in percentages is not. In 1900, Afro-Americans constituted less than 1 percent of the nation's legal professionals; in 1970, they provided only 1.3 percent; and in 1980, they were all of 2.6 percent.

However, there are indications that the percentages of ebon barristers will increase, but these increases will be negligible, and certainly not proportionate to the nation's black population. In 1981, there were over 5,500 blacks studying law constituting 4.4 percent of the 125,000 such students, though their percentage had dwindled from 4.7 percent in 1976. This shrinkage was itself apparently related to charges of "reverse discrimination" in affirmative action programs. Furthermore, the prospective expansion of the black legal profession is threatened by state bar examinations, which a disproportionate number of blacks fail. Indeed, the National Bar Association estimated in 1973 that three out of every four black applicants did not pass this professional admissions hurdle, though they may reapply. This glaring failure rate and the resultant outcry have goaded some jurisdictions to question the administration of their bar tests. Points were found at which race discrimination could pervert the process.

Nevertheless, many states still require, for example, that photographs of the prospective lawyer accompany his test papers.

Afro-Americans are not only underrepresented in law enforcement positions, but in political offices as well. Though extensive politicking in both the North and South has netted a numerical increase in black public servants, their percentages remain small.

In the ten-year period from 1970 to 1980, the numbers of elected black officials throughout the nation increased threefold, moving from less than 1,500 to over 5,000. Even so, they barely exceed 1 percent of the half-million elected American officials. While blacks constitute almost 12 percent of the population, they constitute zero percent of United States senators and 3.5 percent of United States congressmen. At the state and local levels, less than 5 percent of all state legislators; less than 2 percent of all elected municipal officers; and less than 1 percent of all county servants are Afro-Americans. The election of blacks to big-city mayoralties has generated much publicity; yet less than 3 percent of the mayors of towns with a population of over 2,500 had black mayors. The percentages for school boards are also minuscule. Even high-level appointive local posts, such as police and fire chiefs and directors of finance, planning, and public works, are almost exclusively white, ranging from 3 percent to less in black occupants.

The overrepresentation of blacks in crime statistics, and their underrepresentation in law enforcement and political offices, are to a degree reflections of their general economic conditions. At the nation's birth, the United States Constitution stipulated that each black slave be assessed as three fifths of a person; and even this generosity was a compromise of disputes over taxes and congressional representation. However, almost two centuries later, the per capita income of blacks still hovers around three fifths that of whites.

There have of course been improvements in the lives of blacks in the quarter-century since the Montgomery bus boycott of 1955. These advances have generally been unstable ones and suffered particularly from the waging inflation that characterized the 1970s. For instance, in constant 1977 dollars, white families enjoyed an almost 5 percent increase in median income in the 1970-78 period; while blacks suffered a loss of 2.4 percent. By 1978, the median income of black families was less than three fifths that of whites, though it had peaked at 61 percent almost a decade earlier. Almost two fifths of Afro-American families were in the lowest fifth of family incomes, but less than one fifth of Euro-Americans were. Blacks were three times as likely as whites to be classified as poor or near-poor, though in absolute numbers there were over twice as many impoverished whites as blacks. Moreover, the higher up the income ladder you go, the fewer blacks you encounter. For instance, over one fifth of all whites but less than one tenth of all blacks were in the top fifth of family incomes.

The general economic deprivations of Afro-Americans are matched by their paucity in prestige professionals. As seen with legal professionals, blacks have made dramatic gains in the last few years but still their faces are noticeably few among occupational elites. One study of 1,700 senior executives, the *Wall Street Journal* reported in 1980, found only three blacks. A canvass of the Chicago corporate scene by the Urban League uncovered only 117 black heads out of 13,000 managers. Moreover, black executives were likely to be concentrated in personnel and public relations positions, which are not notable launching pads for the top corporate jobs. However, since white executives had been with their companies for longer periods and since there were a number of blacks at the level of assistant vice-president and assistant treasurer, there were signs that the black presence among private executives will increase.

An examination of other occupations evinces the same ambivalence seen in the executive suites. From 1972 to 1979, according to the Census Bureau, the percentages of nonwhites among accountants increased from 4.3 percent to 8.4 percent; among office managers from 1.0 to 2.2; among stock and bond salesmen from 2.0 to 3.3; among bank officers and finance managers from 2.6 to 5.0 (though by 1979 the five largest banks in majority-black Atlanta did not have a single black vice-president out of almost 400 such officers); among wholesale and retail buyers from 4.3 to 6.5; among manufacturing sales representatives from 1.5 to 3.0; among blue-collar supervisors from 6.0 to 7.4; among engineers from 3.4 to 6.3 (though blacks were 2 percent, Hispanics 1 percent and Asian-Americans 4 percent of all physical scientists); among school administrators from 8.2 to 11.6; among registered nurses from 8.2 to 11.4; among medical and osteopathic physicians from 8.2 to 9.5; among lawyers and judges from 1.9 to 2.6 (though the 50 largest law firms had only 12 blacks out of 3,700 partners and furthermore, only one had two black lawyers). Since the Census Bureau included nonblack minority groups in its data, the black percentages in each occupation are less than this recitation would denote. The large gains in minority achievement in the last few years are commendable, but the small percentages remain distressing. The general occupational rule of thumb is—the better the pay, the fewer the blacks.

The private sector is not alone in its racially disproportionate employment practices; the public sector at all levels is included as well. Though the government has surpassed private industry in hiring blacks, it is only a marginal improvement. As with private industry, the occupational rule of thumb is applicable here. By the summer of 1979, for instance, blacks were 16.1 percent of the two and a half million federal civilian employees. Yet the average pay for blacks in the General Schedule (GS) was significantly below all groups, except Native Americans. The average annual income for Native Americans was $11,800; for blacks—$12,100; for Hispanics—$13,200; for Orientals—$15,400; and for whites—$15,340. In other federal pay systems, the disparities are about the same. For example, in the Postal System, which is a fifth black and a long-time bastion of black employment, Afro-Americans earned less than two thirds of the salaries of their white co-workers. Even holding age, education, and previous experience constant, blacks take home substantially smaller federal salaries (an average of $1,700) than whites. Blacks are apparently not being promoted as rapidly as whites. And finally, one study found that, all things being equal, blacks receive 14 percent less in wages than whites in federal, 5 percent less in state, and 8 percent less in local systems, versus 12 percent less on the average in the private sector. The highest measured racial discrimination in wages for all levels of government was at the federal level, and even this was higher than that of private industry. The federal government, widely perceived as the evangelist for racial justice, appears to be backsliding.

If blacks are to improve their economic and political status, they are often urged to excel in education. But the record here is comparable to that in occupations. While Afro-Americans have considerably narrowed the educational gap separating them from whites, the rule of thumb is the more the education, the fewer the blacks. A comparison of the education of the civilian labor force in the late 1970s showed that whites 16 years and older predominate at the high end of the spectrum and blacks at the low end. Over a third of all whites had a year or more of college, while over a fifth of all blacks had an equivalent amount. And this is so even though the number of blacks attending college has doubled since 1968 and now comprise almost a tenth of all college students. Moving to the low end of the scale, blacks were almost twice as likely as whites to have eight or less years of formal education. Indeed, there are allegations, reminiscent of those in crime enforcement, that black students are more quickly suspended and expelled from public secondary schools than their white cohorts.

The comparative differentials between whites and blacks seen across a host of subjects are just as acute in childcare. While two thirds to three quarters of white children between the ages of one and four had been immunized in 1977 against measles, rubella, diphtheria, and tetanus, and had been given three or more doses against polio, only from two fifths to slightly over half of such black children had.

A spate of news stories can illustrate the diverse sources of the plight of black Americans even now, and furthermore, can illuminate the pivotal importance of the law in American society. Although blacks comprise a fifth of the population of Statesville, North Carolina, as of May 1980, none of the town's 57 police and none of the 58 firefighters were black. Under pressure by the United States Department of Justice, the city governors agreed to hire blacks until they are 18 percent of each unit. Moving North, in June 1980, twelve New Jersey cities consented to fill a set proportion of their firefighter vacancies with blacks and Hispanics until minority representation in each city's fire department is equal to the minority percentage of its labor force. Under suit brought by the Department of Justice, each municipality concurred in the quotas, which ranged from 33 percent in Elizabeth to 60 percent in Newark and East Orange.

Private discrimination is just as pervasive though more subtle than public bias. Following modern corporate ritual, Amoco denied in April 1980 that it had discriminated against black and Hispanic credit-card applicants, but promised not to do it again. The Justice Department suit, filed on behalf of the Federal Trade Commission, alleged that the oil company made it difficult for applicants residing in certain postal zones, heavily black and Hispanic ones, to obtain credit cards. In addition, a recent study uncovered the fact that blacks are more likely to be refused mortgages than whites with the same income. If their applications are granted, moreover, they are likely to pay higher interest rates than comparably situated whites.

On the union side of the fence, there were blacks in only 15 percent of the top 800 appointive positions in the United Auto Workers, though blacks were 30 percent of the union's membership. These facts were reported in August 1980 in a suit brought by 18 auto workers who were black, though one union source countered that black apathy at the local level units was the source for the disparity. And in November 1979, there were 280 blacks in a 7,000-member construction union in the eastern Pennsylvania-Delaware region. A federal district judge ordered the union to hire one black for every white in the next two years, with the condition that the quota would be lifted when the percentage of blacks in the union equals the minority population in the two-state metropolitan area. The judge, a black who had retained special jurisdiction of the case after being named to the federal appeals court, also mandated that subcontractors hire blacks on their own if the union cannot make them available.

This dreary litany of statistics and consent decrees could continue, but the dismal picture has been sketched. Even with recent advances, black Americans suffer from crime, poverty, undereducation, and powerlessness. Black judges see these statistics become discrete and incarnate everyday in their courtrooms. The Afro-American jurist is among the elite of his race and the elite of his profession. He is also among the most powerful of his race and of his profession. "If the battleground against racism has shifted to the trial courts," one black jurist has declared, "the chief artillery has to be the judge himself. . . One sure remedy for everyday racist and classist occurrences in our courts is to have more trial judges who are black and/or nonconformist and who are not afraid to use the authority of their office." By evoking race and fear, this commentator highlights the dilemma confronting the black judiciary. On one side, it is to what extent will black judges use their position to correct over three centuries of racism, especially as it manifests itself in the court system. On the other side, it is to what extent will they adopt the role of restraint that is held by their mostly white professional colleagues. This is the choice facing black judges.

Of the judges under study here, over 95 percent sit on trial benches. Though the remainder are appellate jurists, this does not preclude the quandary of race versus robe. We will examine the racial and professional influences on Afro-American judges through their backgrounds, recruitments, and role perceptions. While the performance of their judicial duties will not be scrutinized, there are those who argue that attitudes influence actions. We will thus be able to speculate on the performance of black judges.

RELATED POLITICAL SCIENCE LITERATURE

In considering the background, recruitment, and role perceptions of black judges, this study will relate to three distinct but overlapping subfields of political science: judicial backgrounds; role theory; and black political officials, most especially black jurists.

Studies of the backgrounds of judges are now new. They are at least as old as Beveridge's examination of Chief Justice John Marshall. Almost all of them seek to relate socioeconomic and political background of each jurist to his behavior on the bench. The assumption has been that the judge is a product of this experiences and that a knowledge of certain background factors may be essential to understanding behavior on the bench.

Collective judicial portraits have taken their place along with biographies of individual judges as popular focuses for political science scrutiny and the attributes examined generally remain the same. Schmidhauser, for instance, has sketched a portrait of the justices of the United States Supreme Court. Sheldon Goldman has studied the backgrounds of federal appellate judges, seeking a relationship between background factors and decisional tendencies. In this and later works, he discovered that most of the background factors observed could not be directly related to judicial voting behavior. Yet party affiliation was moderately related to certain kinds of issues, as were age and religion.

Subsequently, Howard focused on the functions of three federal appellate circuits, tracking 5,000 appeals over a twenty-year span. He sought the systemic attributes that bind the highly decentralized federal judiciary, the controls on the discretion of judges, and the methods of maintaining the quality of judicial decisions under heavy volume pressure. He found among other things that (1) federal appeals judges had similar political and especially professional experiences; (2) their socialization for the bench was anticipatory, self-selective, and often professional in basis; (3) the judicial recruitment process tended to weed out incompetents, mavericks, and extremists; (4) they were united by a common understanding of the central mission of their courts as adjudicating agents of the national government; and (5) there was no evidence that uniform role structure controls American judges.

Federal appellate judges are not the only bench members studied. Vines has scrutinized the backgrounds of southern federal district court judges and their decisions in civil rights cases. He discovered relationships between environmental factors (such as birthplace) and judicial decisions. However, Dolbeare studied the backgrounds and behavior of federal district court jurists in metropolitan areas. Federal trial judges were found to be minor actors in urban policy decisions, though state judges were more influential. Nagel, on the other hand, has published a series of articles that examined the relationship between political and ethnic affiliations and the judicial behavior of federal judges.

Though the federal judiciary has been extensively mined, state and local courts contain a motherlode of topics that has been only moderately exploited. Canon has examined the backgrounds and career patterns of state supreme court judges. He found that they were virtually all white, predominantly Anglo-Saxon, Protestants, and overwhelmingly male. Furthermore, over half had worked in the local prosecutor's office at some point in their careers; almost a fifth had served in the office of attorney general; and a fifth had been elected to the state legislature. The backgrounds of local trial judges have also been examined, quite often in connection with recruitment. The Missouri Plan sought to lessen the influence of political parties by authorizing the circumscribed governor to appoint judges, who later run for retention in a plebiscite. Provoked by this reform measure, Watson and Downing compared the backgrounds and decisions of judges selected under the Missouri Plan with those elected to their benches. They found very little difference, though Missouri Plan-judges enjoyed the higher esteem of the state bar and were slightly more likely to be affiliated with the majority political party. Henderson and Sinclair, in their study of Texas jurists, discovered that half had spent more than half of their pre-judicial career in some form of public office, with many coming from the prosecutor's office and from the state legislature. Party activity was the rule for most of their subjects. According to Ish, selected California and Maryland trial judges were also found to be active party members, though the latter were more likely to be politically active.

Judicial recruitment is one of the factors that many background studies have examined. The general findings are similar to those from other background factors: judges are selected from among political party activists. This was true for federal appointive as well as state appointive and elective benches. Bar associations were found to have a greater influence in officially appointive judiciaries, at the federal and state levels, than for elective positions. While many judgeships are officially elective, there are in fact often appointive. This, in turn, causes a shift from politics of the electorate to that of the appointing officer. Finally, law enforcement offices are significant stepping stones to the judiciary, from the United States Supreme Court down to local trial courts. These findings on judicial background and recruitment, especially as they focus on state judiciaries, will be useful in our consideration of the black bench.

The study of attitudes has been closely related to that of background. Background experiences shape attitudes which, in turn, mold behavior. While some students have sought patterns of behavior and deduced attitudes from them, most have focused on role perceptions and then compared them to performance.

The plethora of role perception studies ranges from legislature to judiciaries. The major work in this field is the pioneering effort of Wahlke and others. On the basis of interviews of almost all legislators in four states, they were able to analyze the role perceptions of their subjects in diverse substantive areas. They reported on state legislators' views of the goals of the legislative process; of their constituents; and of interest groups. They concluded that the distribution of role types was related to the idiosyncrasies of each state's political system.

This use of role perceptions to examine legislatures spawned numerous other studies. For instance, Davidson found that selected congressmen were torn between competing roles: getting reelected through close attention to the needs of their constituents as opposed to becoming institutional powers through the acquisition of expert knowledge. Huitt and Matthews each analyzed the folk mores of the Senate and declared that there are informal rules that senators expect their colleagues to obey.

State legislatures have not been neglected. Patterson posited three types of deviant roles after discovering that Wisconsin lawmakers expected adherence to party voting, discouraged overtalking on the floor, and disapproved of pan-handling of lobbyists. Focusing on the Dade County delegation to the Florida legislature, Dauer determined that role perceptions would change as the delegation went from multi-member to single-member districts. Similar studies at the local level have been undertaken, as Zisk, Eulau, and Prewitt have considered the attitudes of selected California city councilpersons. Among other things, they found that their subjects did not consider themselves to be interest group representatives.

While roles have uses in numerous fields, they are particularly appropriate for a study of the judiciary. The judge is one of the most role-conscious of public positions; he is expected to be objective, impartial, precedence-oriented, and indifferent to partisan political activity. Indeed, many students have parted the judge's purple curtain and found the judiciary to be a fertile field for studies of roles.

While Grossman has established the importance of judicial restraint on the behavior of United States Supreme Court Justice Felix Frankfurter, other scholars have studied groups of judges. Glick compared state supreme court justices in four states, attempting to relate their role perceptions to role expectations as given in traditional literature and to judicial behavior. He found differences in perceptions to expectations and perceptions to actual behavior. Later, Glick united with Vines in an effort to relate three role types to actual judicial performance. They used the types of law-interpreter, lawmaker, and pragmatist to explain specific outcomes in cases involving liberal or conservative views. They found that the role types did not explain the outcome of each case.

But Rich was more successful in his study of the federal judges of the Court of Appeals for the Fifth Circuit. He concluded that there were close relationships between background factors, role perceptions, and the voting behavior of his subjects. His study was crippled, however, by a very small sample—seventeen nonunanimous cases.

Impressed by the efforts of Glick, Vines, and Rich, Wold discussed the internal procedures, role perceptions, and judicial behavior, of twenty-four judges of the courts of last resort in four eastern states. His subjects' role perceptions were related to their bench behavior at two points. For example, judges with positive attitudes toward dissent did so more often than those with negative views. Wold further found that, of all background factors studied, only personal political ideology related to role perceptions. Political conservatives adopted the law-interpreter view; moderates the eclectic position; and liberals the lawmaker orientation. Finally, there was no one widely accepted perception of the judicial role.

These studies of role perception focused on federal and state appellate judges and nonjudicial public officials. But Ish shifted to local trial judges to assess role orientations. Examining selected California and Maryland respondents, he found that the vast majority described their judicial role as that of law-interpreter; a much smaller number chose the lawmaker role; and a significant number opted for a position between those two. One implication of his findings was that believers in judicial restraint were more likely to sit on suburban benches.

All of these efforts to weigh the influence of certain role perceptions will be helpful, since the role attitudes of black judges form an important part of our discussion. The Ish study will be especially valuable because most of our respondents are also local trial judges.

The small number of studies of the black public officials partially reflects their general absence from public office. Wilson's discussion of the different styles of Congressmen Adam Clayton Powell of New York and William Dawson of Chicago was for a long period the standard work in this field. But since there has been an increase in the number of black public officials, there has been a corresponding increase in research studies. For example, Conyers and Wallace published the results of a nationwide survey of almost 800 black state, county, and city officeholders. The authors analyzed their subjects' background, for example, their political affiliations and beliefs and their motivations for seeking office. They also sampled 484 white officeholders on many of these same dimensions. In general, it was found that blacks sought office in order to correct social injustices, while whites did so to serve their country. The blacks tended to see more social distinctions among Americans, whereas whites saw "one nation, indivisble."

While some of the findings by Conyers and Wallace will be of value in our examination of black judges, Perry's consideration of black Missouri state legislators is even more useful. Comparing his thirteen subjects with their white fellow legislators during the 1969-70 session, he found that the two groups were similar in many respects: both were long-time residents of their districts; had extensive political backgrounds; and had become politically active at an early age. But the two groups were dissimilar in some ways: the blacks had not achieved the levels of formal education or occupation of their white counterparts. Perry concluded that the black legislators were moderates rather than militants, were cognizant of their race in their legislative duties, were not well integrated into the Missouri legislature, and were not, as a group, a cohesive source of power or influence within the legislative process.

Stone investigated the social origins of the black political elite in Michigan to ascertain their social bias. An analysis of elite backgrounds can, for one, illuminate the impact of societal values on the political recruitment process. Using open-end interviews with 119 blacks holding elective office in Michigan, the author found that her respondents came overwhelmingly from poor families. For example, almost 80 percent of their fathers and almost 90 percent of their mothers were blue-collar workers. In addition, the parents were poorly educated—only a third of the fathers finished high school and only a tenth completed college. These Michiganders were self-made, well-educated, middle-class persons, leading her to conclude that "the civil rights movement only benefited the black middle class and those poised to enter it."

Literature on black lawyers has not been as meager as that on black officeholders. While the black share of the national total of legal professionals has historically been small in percentage figures, it has been numerous enough to earn the attention of a few scholars. Although one of the earliest of these, a small chestnut by Styles in the early 1930s, extolled past and current effort of black lawyers to enhance the rights of blacks, most studies since then have focused their analyses on the economic and legal background of members of the black bench. For instance, in the 1930s, Woodson found that Afro-American lawyers were likely to come from working-class backgrounds; to have problems in establishing a legal practice; and to have difficulty in becoming judges. He estimated that there were no more than a dozen black judges in the country. Almost a quarter of a century later, Edwards, a student of Woodson, reached similar conclusions. But he did note some changes. The younger black lawyers were not as likely to come from working-class homes and did not have as much trouble in establishing a legal practice, though this was still a worry for many.

While the class origins of the black bar appears to have changed even more in recent years, the traditional plaint of establishing a practice remains. Marian S. Goldman concluded, from her study of the black bar in Chicago, that almost two thirds of the attorneys examined came from marginally bourgeois backgrounds. But even some black lawyers trained at top quality law schools often had trouble putting their legal practice on firm foundations. A number of them received state governmental positions of limited power and remained in these jobs until they had built their clientele and reputations to a sufficient level to begin full-time private practice. The lack of legal business forced many black practitioners to become involved in local politics. Goldman's findings are interesting yet they are qualified by the small size of her sample—only twenty respondents.

The results of survey research have provided much of what is currently known about the black bench, though individual jurists have provided some insights into their own experiences and expectations. Jerome Schuman conducted a national survey of the black bar and bench in 1971. Through questionnaires and some in-depth interviews, he probed the backgrounds, careers, and education of 800 black lawyers and 50 black judges. He deduced that black lawyers earned less than their more numerous white cohorts because of the effects of racism in American life. While Schuman's study suffered from a two-prong focus and a relatively low response, it did provoke others to examine the black legal profession. Somewhat later, *Judicature* conducted a survey of black judges exclusively and had a more acceptable response rate of over 60 percent. This study found that many of the respondents had been born in the South; four fifths had been affiliated with all-black law firms; political involvement had been high, with two thirds describing themselves as politically active before coming on the bench; two thirds were appointed to their judgeships; no single career route predominated, though many had been in the prosecutor's office at some point; and, while a minute percentage described themselves as politically conservative, almost three fifths considered themselves liberals.

In another national survey of Afro-American jurists, Cook analyzed thirty-seven states with a large enough black population to justify black judicial representation. While black judges were underrepresented in all the states, some states were worse than others. An inverse relationship was found in both the South and the North: the greater the state's black population, the lesser its black judicial population. It was more difficult for blacks to ascend to the judiciary in strong one-party, mostly southern, states than in competitive two-party and weak one-party states. Cook further found indications that a city's level of black judicial representation paralleled its level of school segregation. Cook can be commended for her provocative conclusions, but faulted for her imprecise statement of themes and haphazard writing.

Uhlman's comparative analysis is the most recent one on black judges. Provoked by numerous findings of racial disparities in sentencing, he sought to assess the impact of black judges in the criminal sanctioning process in one urban jurisdiction. His data included the backgrounds of 16 black and 79 white judges and the disposition of 42,000 criminal cases during a six-year period.

Uhlman found that background differences between black and white judges were small. Their pre-judicial careers paralleled each other, with local ties and high quality legal training being important for both. There were few group differences in the sentencing of black and white defendants by black and white judges. Yet there were differences among individual judges. Overall, race and other background factors were found to have weak relationships with sanctioning behavior. While black and white defendants were convicted at approximately the same rate, blacks were given harsher sentences than whites. The more serious charges against blacks accounted for a quarter of the interracial sentencing differences. Furthermore, black defendants fared poorly at important intermediate stages of the criminal process, which affected the ultimate disposition of their cases. For example, blacks failed to make bail more often than whites and were more likely to be represented by court-appointed attorneys. The remaining 40 percent of the sentencing disparity between black and white defendants could not be explained and may represent evidence of racial discrimination by both black and white judges.

The scope and methodology of Uhlman's study are laudable. Yet his conclusions that black judges as a group sentenced at approximately the same rate as whites and that there may be some racial discrimination in the sentencing disparities uncovered, must be disquieting to those who thought that black judges would have a greater impact upon the legal system. A flaw in his analysis may be his assumptive grouping of black judges. There are differences in race sensitivity among blacks as well as whites, and he did find *individual* differences in sanctioning. The individuals and their backgrounds were not disclosed. In our consideration of the factors that influence the role perceptions of Afro-American black judges, we seek to isolate certain background variables that may undergird judicial performance and may help sensitize the American judiciary to racial discrimination.

Having placed our examination of black jurists in the context of American racial realities and in the context of political science literature, we must now discuss methodology before proceeding to our research findings.

Chapter 2
Design and Method

Race is one of the basic distinctions of American society. This distinction is older than the American Republic and has had a great impact upon all who have lived with it. The existence of the nation itself was tested most severely in a civil war fueled by racial distinctions. Hundreds of thousands of persons were killed and the lives of many millions more were changed by this armed conflict. Yet the affect of racial differences was not isolated to one major military campaign. Individual racial skirmishes have been frequent events: the slave rebellions of the 1800s; bloody Kansas of the 1850s; the Draft Riots of 1863; the lynching of thousands of blacks until the 1950s; the post-World War I and World War II riots; and the urban disturbances of the 1960s. All of these traumatic occurrences and many more have pockmarked American history. Conflict, however, has not been the only result of racial differences. Political, economic, and social disparities have also ensued. Black Americans collectively have less political power and are less affluent than white Americans.

As extensive as racism is, black Americans have improved their economic and political status in the past quarter-century. For instance, between 1968 and 1980, the number of black political officeholders tripled. Among these 5,000 ebon public servants are approximately 500 judicial officers. Since Afro-American jurists in such quantity are recent additions to the American polity, the few studies that have been conducted have confined themselves to descriptions of backgrounds or comparisons of the sanctioning behavior of a small sample of black and white judges. Certainly, there has not been a perceptual study of black judges as a whole. Our goal is to trace the influence of diverse agents, including race and professionalism, on the lives of black judges and to assess the weight of these factors on perceptions of judicial duties.

Our research design is divided into two parts. First, we will examine the backgrounds of our subjects. This trek will carry us from a consideration of family status and socialization in law and politics to judicial recruitment and civil rights activity. Second, we will correlate selected background factors with judicial role perceptions to ascertain the impact of different factors on their job-related attitudes.

Among the most powerful members of their race, Afro-American judges are especially ripe for study. Many of the political and economic conflicts involving black Americans are eventually brought to the courts for resolution. Black jurists are in a position to help redress past and present racial inequities. They may do this in individual cases but their rulings can influence actors beyond the individual litigants immediately before them. They can determine the "rules of the game" by deciding the content and scope of constitutions—federal and state; of statutes—federal, state, and city; and of administrative rules and regulations.

Assumptions are made in most human activities. Though they may be realized or unrealized, they exist nevertheless. There are at least two major assumptions made in this study. (1) Scrutinizing the personal characteristics of black judges will help us understand their attitudes. Such background studies are not new and have taken many different forms. Our examination is primarily a descriptive type; as much information as is possible is gathered in order to elucidate the state of mind of our subjects. (2) Though racism is extensive and affects all Americans, its impact varies from person to person. This study assumes that the force of racial discrimination will have different degrees of impact on black judges. There is evidence for making this assumption. Schuman and Hatchett have found that certain factors (such as age, education, income, and occupation) are related to the degree of black alienation from the American political system. The affect of race also varies with whites. Campbell discovered that the white population exhibited a wide range of feelings toward blacks. A fifth to a third of his respondents were generally positive in their racial outlook; tended to accept interracial contact; were sensitive to racial discrimination; and were sympathetic to various forms of black protest. On the other hand, an equal proportion of whites were found to have negative or even hostile feelings toward blacks.

Having stated the assumptions underlying this study, we shall now define its boundaries.

(1) This is a descriptive survey of all black judges who responded to our structured questionnaire (see Appendix). Our respondents preside over federal and state, and appellate and trial courts. Most, however, sit on state trial benches. Our focus could have been narrowed to include only these subjects; this might have been better for comparative purposes. Yet we seek the influence of race and judicial role upon all black judges, and judicial distinctions do not hinder that search.

(2) This is a collective portrait of Afro-American jurists, not of any one individual. Our findings of the impact of race upon background and role perceptions apply only to the general group, not to the individuals who compose the collective.

(3) This is an examination of the role perceptions of incumbent actors, not of behavior or even role itself.

(a) Though Glick and Vines and others have assumed that a "knowledge of basic attitudes and perceptions held by public officeholders can provide a basis for understanding some patterns of behavior among officials," our study does not contain data enabling us to assess behavior. Since some students have maintained that attitudes and expectations can be *indicators* of behavior, we will attempt such an extrapolation here.

(b) One widely used method of ascertaining attitudes and expectations is the concept of role. But it is an imprecise instrument, and much of this imprecision originates in the variety of definitions employed. Many of these clarifications try to accommodate the systemic position as well as the individual personality. For instance, Grossman characterized role as a "consistent pattern of behavior on the part of an individual in response to *his* conception of the nature of his function in a system." Mitchell, however, defines it simply as "the interplay between organizational structure and personality." Yinger argues that a term is needed to refer to "that part of the self which represents a given individual's tendencies to perform a role in a given way."

(c) In our study, role perception is defined as an individual's tendency to see his role in a given way. We will be describing a collective of individual role perceptions, not behavior or role.

DATA COLLECTION

Our consideration of Afro-American jurists will use two methods for collecting data: mailed questionnaires and personal interviews. These two methods will allow for a fuller, more balanced description of the respondents, since they complement each other. Questionnaires allow us to survey the universe of jurists, afford some uniformity of standards, give greater confidence of anonymity, and place less pressure on the subject to respond. On the other hand, since a questionnaire demands writing, usually in constricted space, the personal interview is used to clarify the ambiguities of the written responses. The interview, as Dexter explains, is a "more appropriate technique for revealing information about complex, emotionally laden subjects as for probing the sentiments which may underlie an expressed opinion."

A listing of black judicial officials, as of August 1972, was obtained from the Judicial Council of the National Bar Asscoation; it contained 288 names. A questionnaire, consisting of nine pages and thirty-eight, mostly structured questions, was sent to the judges. Most of the questions could be checked off, though some respondents added extensive comments. There were three mailings, extending over a period of two and a half months, from November 1972, through mid-January 1973. The first complete mailing (three cover letters and the questionnaire) garnered 100 responses; a follow-up, reminding letter resulted in

50 more responses; and a second complete mailing resulted in another 35 answers. A total of 185 judges replied, for a response rate of 64 percent (185 out of 288). A Chicagoan wrote that he had spent thirty years trying to erase color distinctions and would not answer any questionnaire based upon such distinctions. One New Yorker was affronted because he received a form letter. He, too, did not return the questionnaire.

Of the respondents, nine are appellate judges; the rest sit on trial benches. Over 91 percent preside at the state level, with the remainder occupying federal seats. Also, there are two Puerto Ricans and two Virgin Islanders among these jurists.

In order to amplify the responses from the mailed questionnaire, personal interviews with eleven judges were conducted from late October to early December 1973. Interviews were requested with twelve of the respondents and only one refused, giving a 91 percent response rate. The subjects were chosen on the basis of convenience; yet an inspection of the distribution of all respondents indicates that the interviewees were generally representative. All were state trial judges, though one also had appellate jurisdiction; four were on appointive benches and seven were on elective ones, though only two were initially elected; while only one was a non-Easterner, all sat in large urban jurisdiction; three were Republicans; their ages ranged from one 75-year-old to a pair of 39-year-olds, with most in their 40s ands 50s; and, finally, one was female. All interviews were taped in the judges' chambers, except one in which the author speedily drove a visiting judge to a departing airplane.

On the basis of the survey and interviews, we describe background factors in chapters 3 through 6, while chapter 7 is a discussion of the racial and judical world view of black judges. All five chapters utilize simple percentages to depict the alignment of the subjects across an array of factors. The remaining chapters discuss the correlations of background factors with role perceptions. This is done to gauge the impact of race and judicial role among other variables on the judges' views of their judicial duties.

Before discussing the findings, a methodological note on the last chapters is necessary. Most of the correlations involve ordinal or sequential level variables and will rely upon Kendall's Tau b or c to measure statistical significance as well as strength and direction of the observed relationships. Kendall's Tau b is appropriate for square tables—those in which the number of rows equals the number of columns. Kendall's Tau c, on the other hand, is necessary for rectangular tables—those in which the number of rows differs from the number of columns. In addition, a lesser number of the correlations involve nominal level variables and will rely upon chi-square to determine statistical significance; Cramer's V will measure the strength of such relationships, though phi as a gauge of strength occasionally surfaces. We will accept as statistically significant relationships that have a probability of occurring by chance 5 percent of the time or less (.05). This is the conventioal social science standard. As a test of association, Kendall's Tau b or c has a value range of 0 to ± 1, with the distance from 0 indicating strength and plus or minus denoting direction of such relationships. Cramer's V has a range of 0 to + 1 and only measures strength of associations. Finally, some categories of variables have been collapsed or discarded for statistical reasons, usually because of low response rates. Such actions will be inndicated in the appropriate places.

Starting with background facts, we now turn to that staple of social science research—family status.

Chapter 3
Social and Political Backgrounds of Black Judges

It seems that black Americans have always had an affinity for the North. It was for a long time the nearest refuge from the violence and cruelty of Southern slavery. After slavery was officially abolished by the Emancipation Proclamation, a few blacks continued the trek northward, but the migration began in earnest at the start of World War I. This black migratory pattern, from the South to the North, from the farm to the city, has been well noted and is mirrored in the black judges under study here.

The most striking feature in their geographical backgrounds is the number of judges who were born in the South but who now preside in the North. Combining the areas of the Deep South (Louisiana, Mississippi, Alabama, Florida, Georgia, and South Carolina) and the Outer South (North Carolina, Virginia, West Virginia, Kentucky, Tennessee, Arkansas, Oklahoma, and Texas), over half—51 percent—of the respondents were born in that region. Almost a fifth (18 percent) were natives of the Upper Atlantic region of Pennsylvania, New Jersey, and New York. No other section proved to be as fertile. For instance, approximately a tenth of each group were born in the Midwest (stretching from Ohio to Wisconsin) and in the Rocky Plains states, mostly Missouri. Four percent or less of the black bench originated in the Mid-Atlantic zone (from the District of Columbia to Delaware), New England, and the Far West, mostly California.

These jurists, like many of their race fellows, emigrated from the South to other parts of the country. For some the move came early. Though over half were born in the South, less than a third (32 percent) were reared there. This decrease can be seen in the increases in other regions, most notably the Upper Atlantic and the Midwest (26 and 17 percent, respectively). While the Rocky and Plains area retained its tenth, 7 percent each were nurtured in the states of the Mid-Atlantic and the Far West, with 3 percent finding sanctuary in New England.

The southern configuration becomes even more pronounced when one looks at the present location of members of the ebon bench. The South has only a tenth of the respondents; the heavily industrialized Upper Atlantic states have almost a third (32 percent) of the total; the Midwest, also well industrialized, has over a fifth (22 percent); and the Far West, primarily California, has 15 percent of all black judges in the country. Slightly less than a tenth each rule in the Mid-Atlantic and the Rocky and Plains states (9 and 8 percent, respectively), while dependable New England maintains its 3 percent. Even so, this concentration of black jurists in northern urban areas should not be too surprising since three fourths of black Americans live in metropolitan areas and almost half reside in the North and West.

The black migration from the South involved both a push and pull motion. The "push" came from the South with its precarious existence for the black sharecropper, low wages, high debts, frequent agricultural adversities, and blatant, violent race bigotry. The North provided the "pull" with its high wages, expanding employment opportunities, quality schools, personal and property protections, and diverse social events. The move northward was primarily an economic one. It is no accident that the greatest concentration of black migrants and subsequently of black judges is in New York, Pennsylvania, Ohio, Illinois, Michigan, and California. These states offered the jobs, the dollars, and the opportunities that beckoned poor southern migrants. That there are now so many black judges presiding in the North suggests that the North may have partially delivered on its promise for some black southerners.

There is a fairly wide range in the ages of these judges at the time of their response to the questionnaire, though over seven tenths are within a twenty-year span—45-64 years of age. Four of the respondents (2 percent) are 34 years or younger and nine (5 percent) are 70 years or older. Indeed, the ages of these jurists on a graph would almost perfectly resemble a bell-shaped curve. They range from 8 percent for 35-39-year-olds; 9 percent for those 40-44; 17 percent for those 45-49; 29 percent for those 50-54; 15 percent for those 55-59; 11 percent for those 60-64; and 6 percent for those 65-69. Since these data contain a sizable number of state trial judges (with only a sprinkling of federal and/or appellate ones), and since most judicial studies have focused on the federal and/or appellate level, there is probably little utility in comparing the age distribution of these judges with most other judicial studies. But the age distribution here is comparable to that found by Henderson and Sinclair in their study of Texas judges, indicating that the age distribution of these black judges may be within the norm for trial court judges. In addition, selected California and Maryland trial judges exhibited approximately the same age range.

In studying black judges one should prepare to be surprised. Because of the peculiar status of blacks in American society, it probably should be expected that a study of black judicial officers would uncover facts quite unlike those found about white judges. The initial surprise was the large number of black judges now presiding in cities to which they had only recently arrived as migrants. This finding was quite unlike the general finding of other judicial studies in that most judges are born and reared in the area in which they are sitting. Furthermore, as a general rule, judgeships are elite positions usually attracting middle- and upper-class natives. That is not true for these black jurists. Slightly more than three fifths of the respondents (62 percent) are from working-class backgrounds. Though somewhat less than a third (32 percent) cited a middle-class background and 6 percent stated that they came from the upper class of their communities, the upper mobility shown by these respondents is very strong.

Education is usually seen as the hallmark of middle-class status in this country. Those claiming such status in this study had parents who were relatively well educated, and they were certainly better educated than the majority of blacks, and even whites, of their generation. Forty-five of their fathers had at least some college training, if not a degree. And an additional four had fathers with a professional and/or graduate training. Fifty-seven had mothers with some college training, and at least one had a mother with a graduate degree. Parental education appears to be the most reliable predictor of middle-class status. But education alone does not account for all of those claiming bourgeois status. Some describing themselves as middle class had parents who had no college education, though they were not very numerous. They tended to be morticians and farmers with extensive landholdings.

Those who came from middle-class backgrounds, and whose parents were relatively well educated, had fathers with comparable occupations: ministers, civil service employees (quite often in the postal system), contractors, realtors, lawyers, doctors, educators, and businessmen and merchants. Some fathers had two jobs, such as lawyer-minister, lawyer-teacher, and teacher-social worker. This was a much more common occurrence among the middle class than among the working class. This two-income characteristic of the black bourgeoisie is prevalent even now, since both husband and wife work.

Of the middle-class mothers, some were simply homemakers, possibly indicative of sizable families. Of those who did work, most were in professional positions: teachers (the most numerous category, as would be expected), nurses, social workers, and bookkeepers. Except for the last profession, each would be within the norm for a middle-class black woman of a generation or more ago.

The mothers of those few claiming upper-class status, like their middle-class counterparts, also worked in professional positions. Furthermore, the upper-class fathers had such occupations as college dean, judge, lawyer, pharmacist, and doctor.

The much more numerous group, those in the working-class ranks, had fathers with blue-collar jobs. They ranged from carpenter to cook to mailroom clerk, from baker to bricklayer to barber, from factory worker to truck driver, from janitor to gardener, and from mechanic to farmer to machinist. A few others professing to working-class status actually had fathers with relatively white-collar, although possibly low-paying, jobs: school principal, accountant, and owner of a bar. The mothers in working-class famijlies, when not simply homemakers, were likely to work as maids or seamstresses, as would be expected.

The large number of black judges with self-described working-class backgrounds raises some questions about the utility of the concept of class when studying black families. Billingsley, in his book *Black Families in White America,* raises the same objections, especially as used by many sociologists, most notably Moynihan. He thinks that the tripartite concept of class—lower, middle, and upper—used by many in comparing white families, cannot be used as fruitfully when studying blacks, because there are too many variations and gradations within the working or lower class for the typology to yield useful results. Of those black judges of working-class origins who were personally interviewed, many in essence described themselves as "respectable lower class," to use one of Billingsley's own phrases. Their parents were religious, hardworking people who pushed their children to get an education and to get ahead. For example, one judge observed of the term *lower class:*

I don't think that term applies to my parents, of that era. . .20 or 25 years ago. There were any number of people during those times who were poor but would be described today as middle class. . . They would say, 'Be clean, work, and you'll get ahead.'

According to one elderly jurist, his father stressed education though he never went to school a day in his life. Finally, another, when asked what values his family instilled in him, replied: "Hard work, be fair, honest. . .get an education, hustle."

It is clear that these judges do not fit class stereotypes. Quite possibly these stock images are wrong for blacks, and maybe for whites, as well.

In addition, the class makeup and education of the parents of black judges may distinguish them from other black public officials, such as legislators. Investigating Afro-American public officeholders in the state of Michigan, Stone found that 80 percent of the fathers and 90 percent of the mothers of her respondents had been blue-collar workers. Two thirds of the fathers had failed to finish high school, and only one tenth were college graduates. Maternal education was even lower—only 5 percent had matriculated from the halls of higher education. While these findings call into question the traditional use of class to define the black community, they suggest moreover that our black judges were especially favored in their backgrounds.

The religious affiliations of the parents of the respondents were probably predictable. Over 46 percent said that their parents were Baptists, with those belonging to the Methodist denominations comprising over a quarter more.

Together these two groups account for approximately 70 percent of the parents. However, it is something of a truism that upwardly mobile people gravitate to institutions that match their newly won status. This axiom seems to have found added substantiation in the religious alegiances of these judges. There is a marked decrease in the number listing themselves as Baptist. Less than a quarter (24 percent) of the respondents remain in the fundamentalist denomination of their mothers and fathers. And Methodist adherents dropped from a quarter of the parents to 15 percent of the children. There is moreover a corresponding rise in the higher-status denominations. For instance, Presbyterian members more than doubled from parents to children, standing at 11 percent of the subjects. Worshippers in the Episcopalian church also jumped considerably, from approximately a tenth of the parents to 16 percent of their offsprings. "The universally well-trained" Episcopal minister was the reason why one judge switched from the Baptist-Methodist faiths of her parents. She added, "I just refuse to believe that one who has not mastered verbs, has mastered the Bible." "Status-seeking" was not the grounds for her denominational change; "it was just trying to get some common level of education."

In addition, the "other" category, often Congregationalist and Lutheran, shows a moderate increase, from 8 to 12 percent. Catholic parishoners move from 8 to 13 percent of the subjects. And there is a curious growth in the number of those claiming no religious preference. Whether this group is composed of nonmember believers, agnostics, or atheists, is not known. But this increase should not be overly surprising since these are highly educated individuals, and more prone to doubt.

POLITICAL SOCIALIZATION

Politics is not simply a matter of written laws and formal institutions. Human behavior is the essential ingredient of any polity. Whether laws will be obeyed, taxes paid, or rulers respected, are only some of the aspects of the extrainstitutional dimension involving human behavior. Attitudes, values, beliefs, and norms, are important because they partially determine the functioning of political society. The process by which people learn these political dispositions and behavior is called political socialization.

Many agents transmit this political information: the family, peer groups, educational institutions, and the mass media. The family has been the most discussed agent of political learning because of its dominant position in the early life of the individual. Even by its most innocent deeds, the family socializes the child to politics. An inspection of the backgrounds of black judges provides further evidence of the political influence of family members.

The transmission of partisan identification from parents to children has been widely documented. For instance, the Democratic party has been the political haven for most blacks since the presidency of Franklin Delano Roosevelt. The party affiliations of these black judges reflects that political allegiance. Almost 70 percent of the respondents claimed to be members of Roosevelt's party, while barely a quarter (27 percent) described themselves as Republicans. Moreover, respondents appear to have followed their parents' lead in their partisan alignment. Over half (55 percent) of the parents were remembered as members or followers of the Democratic party, while 39 percent described their mothers and fathers as Republican faithfuls. But there is a moderate difference in the political party allegiance between parents and children. It is plausible that older black judges were more likely to have had Republican parents. After all, the party of Lincoln and emancipation once claimed the allegiance of black Americans as intensely as the Democratic party of Roosevelt and economic relief does today. In other words, these parents were not merely transmitting a particular party affiliation but a substantive political outlook—advancing the status of black Americans.

The personally interviewed respondents were asked why they were members of their respective political parties. Their answers were not unusual; possibly, they were predictable. Some were members because of the ideological bent of the parties, some because the party was the majority one in their jurisdiction, and others because their friends or parents were members. One hereditary Republican offered this explanation:

> When I got up to the age of reason, I suspect I found intellectual justifications and excuses for being what I already was. If one really analyzes why I am a Republican, I suspect the fundamental reason is that my parents were.

One New Dealer responded:

> I suppose I am a Democrat because I came along in Roosevelt's day. I suppose it's just as simple as that... Then I just liked the more liberal philosophy of the Democratic party.

The liberal philosophy of the Democrats partially explains the gravitation of these black judges to that party. But pragmatism also plays a part, as one long-time Republican asserted:

> The Democratic party at the beginning was a party... that simply had as its objective, ousting the Republican... I can think of no philosophical reasons why I should change. And there was a practical one why I should remain... it was the major party here, I was a favorite son.

This Republican's practical approach to politics is matched on the Democratic side:

> I registered Democrat because many years ago, when I was young, I was advised, and I think it was proper advice by an older man, that since the Democrats almost always got elected in Maryland, if we registered as Democrats, we would have some say-so in the primary elections.

Given the long-term partisan alignment of black Americans, it should not be too surprising that the affiliation of these judges is overwhelmingly Democratic. Yet the percentage of black Republicans on the bench is greater than that of the general black population. Over a quarter of the black bench is aligned with the GOP, but less than a tenth of the Afro-American populace is. Republicans may be overrepresented on the bench because of their ability to win the governorship which, in many states, staffs the judiciary.

Since parents bestow their political party affiliation and possibly their general political orientation upon their children, it should not be surprising that they would also be one of the primary agents shaping their children's interest in politics. Almost a third (30 percent) of the black jurists cited their parents as the initial political influence in their lives. This appears to be within the normal range, since parental influence on the socialization of political activists has been found to be between 30 and 40 percent. Yet the family is not the only socializing agent; peer groups and schools have been recognized for their role in shaping political dispositions. The influence of both is further underlined by our respondents. For instance, over a fifth (22 percent) mentioned a friend as the primary agent for their political interest, and a teacher was the initial agent for 8 percent, and 12 percent cited "other."

Probably the most striking statistic in this analysis is that almost 30 percent of these black judges cited civil rights issues as the primary source of their concern for politics. In fact, the influence of civil rights is almost impossible to isolate; it surfaced in varying degres in the other categories as well. While not usually accorded major status as an agent of political socialization, the influence of issues is not new. Prewitt, in his study of city councilmen, found that over a quarter connected their political interest to social problems. But, given the strong influence of civil rights issues in the political upbringing of these black jurists, it would seem only natural that sensitivity to race would color their judicial philosophies as well.

While there are similarities, the evidence mounts that these black jurists enjoyed indulgences denied other black political elites. For the majority of black public servants in Michigan, political interests were not inherited. Only 17 percent were introduced to politics by their parents. Over half ascribed their earliest governmental awareness to incidents in their neighborhoods. But, in the similarity to black judges, nearly a quarter were provoked by the absence of blacks in government.

One arbiter cited his family, friend, and teacher, as the primary influences on his political interest. Asked if his family discussed politics, he replied, "Yes, it was Franklin D. Roosevelt; this is what they were talking about. And they were talking about Hoover bringing on the depression." The friend, he related, was a lawyer and printer who intensified his political interest through conversations. And of his teacher, he exclaimed:

> The teacher was, oh was he terrific, Charlie Thomas; I never will forget him. He taught civics, government. And he really stimulated my thinking through the area of law and politics because he really delved into it. It wasn't a textbook situation but he really put a lot into it.

Another, whose father weaned him on Roosevelt liberalism, recalled their many political conversations:

> ...most of the political things that were going on, he was quite aware of and talked about constantly. It was nothing for him and I, for instance, after dinner to sit there and just talk about any number of political topics...And as a young person, I enjoyed that considerably...

A number of the personally interviewed judges could remember such incidents with their family. Indeed, 44 percent of all respondents noted that their parents discussed politics with them. For most, such conversations emphasized general political orientations. Political activity was spoken of in a positive and hopeful tone by the parents of 37 percent or 68 of these black judges. One Marylander recounted numerous positive conversations with his politically active parents. He traced his present political optimism to a childhood incident: the gubernatorial victory of a Republican candidate who was "elected on promises given to blacks." As a payoff, blacks "got a list of scholarships and jobs...which we had never had before, which I thought was a real positive thing in those days." The "very positive" political discussions of one father are also currently reflected in the hopeful attitude of his son. Their conversations have "helped" to give me a lot of insight into things that go on now." Such parent-child talks imparted not merely a view of politics, but a view of life as well.

> Yeah, my father was one of these tough guys...His thing was if you worked hard, got out there are hustled, and got in the middle of things, you know, things would go right for you.

Of course, many black families did not discuss politics at all because they were excluded from participation by law or by social circumstances. One former Tennessean recalled that government affairs were "very, very rarely" a topic of conversation when he was a child. Since blacks were completely excluded from local and state offices. . . we had no interest in them, none whatsoever. . . We could not associate positively with any politics because it didn't mean anything to us. We knew politics was for white people and not for black people.

This exclusion has today left a residue of skepticism. Though blacks are now involved in politics, he feels that "somewhere down the line, they are going to be cheated and taken advantage of." Thus, even when not discussing affairs of state, the family has shaped political dispositions.

The influence of parental political interest may, on the other hand, be limited or hindered by the child's mental development. For some, curiosity about government affairs had to await an immediate, concrete provocation. Citing civil rights as his initial agent, one judge did not become interested in politics until college, even though his father was active in community affairs and in civil rights. The provocation was a racial one—the lack of public accommodations for black students. As he explained it,

Certain problems of a racial nature came up from time to time, and the solution to these problems depended on the actions of those who were there on campus, and I tried to rally to the cause, to meet the challenge. . . All of these things (racial discriminations) existed on the campus, and they would not be changed unless we, black students on the campus, did something about it. And we decided to do it as a group.

One ninth of the respondents chose "other" as the primary political influence. Some in this category cited business reasons for their political interest. One jurist noted that "politics in Chicago assists an attorney in getting business," An eastern judge cited "plain common sense, necessity" as the reason for this political interest: "I knew there was no way to change the horrible conditions unless I became active."

This type of answer was not unusual. A wish to influence civic action and to serve the community was the motivating influence for a number of these judges. One westerner, citing community service, stated that he "would not have become politically active except to support a good candidate."

As the family is a dominant influence on political socialization, the formative years of youth are a major period of initial political interest. Over a third of the black bench (34 percent), for example, traced their political curiosity to their childhood. Another 7 percent remembered adolescence as the stage of their initial awareness. The combination constitutes a significant total of the respondents, over two fifths, who have maintained a long-term interest in public affairs. For Prewitt, such people among his councilman were less reluctant to identify with the political component of their position. A comparable relationship may be found among these judges.

Almost a fifth of them (18 percent) developed an awareness of public affairs in college. One jurist noted this phase in his effort to change the segregative practices of his college and its surrounding community. An additional ninth (12 percent) found themselves in law school before their political interests were stimulated. One District of Columbia judge realized while studying law that "to be successful in improving the quality of life that people enjoyed generally. . . I recognized you got to deal with the political forces that prevail in this country." The Young Democrats and the Young Republicans organizations were his lessons. "I saw people bettering their own beds for future employment and future careers" through their party activity. He resolved "to better my own bed."

While political interest began during childhood for many Afro-American jurists, no subsequent period attracted similar numbers until the point of law practice, when over a quarter (27 percent) became curious about government affairs. A racially motivated rejection by a prestigious law firm was the rationale given by an Upper-Atlantic respondent who became politically provoked after he had passed the bar examination. Though this would appear to be relatively late for such an elite to develop such interest, other studies have found comparable patterns. Adult experiences triggered involvement in public affairs for almost 40 percent of elective California councilmen. Furthermore, another tenth became engaged in politics only after their selection to the local governing board. And while a third of black Michigan officeholders were stimulated by government in high school or in previous grades, a quarter were not awakened until they were in their twenties, and a quarter more waited until they were in their thirties.

Almost half of the black bench (48 percent) cited political parties as their initial vehicle into political activity. Some joined political clubs for business reasons, some to work for a particular candidate, and others to improve the plight of blacks in this country.

One Republican first became active when asked to serve as a watcher at elections. But afterward he found that party activity was also good business:

> I became attorney and counsel for the executive committee and personal attorney for the ward leader who was a businessman; then personal attorney later on to the owner. . . of the black newspaper of the city, which was a Republican newspaper.

Casework, now almost frozen in myth and legend as a stereotypical Democratic monopoly, was also practiced by Republicans. A Republican-turned-Democrat indicates how the GOP ward heeler plied his trade:

> I was turned down by this big law firm and I felt so badly. I had nowhere to go. . . I was going to be married in a short while, and I had no money,

nothing. A Negro politician, then's when I got into politics...lived opposite me...(and when) this story came out in the paper that I had been turned down by this big law firm, he got mad. He was precinct captain...came to my house...'I'll take you down to my man,' white man, the leader of the politics of the Republican party in (the city)...

The Republican leader immediately got him a job in his law firm. And thus he began a career-long involvement in both party activity and civil rights. Another party activist felt that "the only way that blacks can see themselves moving along is to get inside and participate and be active in various political processes."

The mixture of motives for the party activists is difficult to untangle but, implicitly and explicitly, one of the motives is a concern for the status of American blacks. Consequently, it is not surprising that over a fifth (22 percent) of these black judges cited the civil rights movement as their initial vehicle into politics. Sixteen percent said that they became active through friends. Here, too, the saliency of race is evident. Through the urging of a friend or law partner, some became active in a particular civil rights campaign or in a black candidate's bid for political office.

Another 14 percent chose "other" when asked to indicate their first political activity. This is a diverse collection, ranging from those who stated that they were never politically active to those whose political activity was motivated by personal employment problems. One appointed judge said that he was "never active, except as a speech-writing prostitute for a favored candidate (generally a loser)." A midwesterner noted that his first political activity was as a nonpartisan candidate for justice of the peace, while an easterner stated that he became involved politically because he needed a clerkship in order to qualify for the bar exams. And then there were those who cited political activity stemming from interest in the community as well as a "commitment to citizenship duties."

While there are diverse reasons as to why these black judges chose different vehicles for their initial political activity, the most persistent theme is that of race consciousness, regardless of vehicle. These respondents express a pervasive awareness of the inferior position of Afro-Americans. This awareness may shape their approach to their judicial duties. Yet, as judges, they are obliged to be fair and objective to all litigants. While trying to eradicate race discrimination, they possibly suffer a basic conflict between the role expected of them by the brothers of their race and by the brethren of their benches.

Though race sensitivity underlies much of the political socialization of Afro-American judges, our general findings agree with prior studies: the child learns about politics mainly from his family. Children do imitate their parents; however, as Jaros phrases it, they "are not fully chips off the old political block." As we have implied, other forces shape the political orientation of each citizen. The impact of these nonfamiliar forces can be more clearly gauged when comparing the political activity of black judges and their parents. Our respondents were perceptibly more engaged in politics than their parents. Only when performing the threshold duty of voting did parents approximate the partisan activity of their children—83 percent of the parents versus 97 percent of the judges voted. But as the political involvement deepened, parental participation lessened. For example, a mere third of the parents were party members. While this may have been high for persons of their generation, three quarters of their children listed themselves on the party rolls. Over half (54 percent) of the jurists were political campaign workers compared to slightly less than a quarter (24 percent) of their parents. And the gap widens: the judges were five times more likely to be party contributors and candidates than their parents. While 49 percent of the respondents had helped fill the party coffers, only 10 percent of their parents had. Though 35 percent of the arbiters had run for public office, just 7 percent of their progenitors had set the example, with four of the thirteen parents winning their races. Indeed, many of these respondents appear to have been seasoned political operatives: approximately 30 percent had been political advisors and party officials. In addition, 13 percent had been campaign managers.

In the United States, according to surveys, the middle and upper classes are more politically active than the working class. The differences in partisan participation between these judges and their parents buttress that observation. While culture may account for the discrepancies, there may be additional contributory factors. The civil rights movement spawned extensive black involvement in public affairs, as well as provoking federal legislation to protect these new participants. Finally, and very importantly, professional necessity may have driven the respondents into the political arena, since law and politics rely upon the same set of skills.

Even so, while families shape their children in many ways, it is obvious that black judges were not fully imitating the civic actions of their parents. Learning political dispositions is a continuous lifelong process. A generational change in attitudes, values, and behavior, seems to have occurred from parents to judges. These well-educated jurists possess different attributes than their less-educated parents. Familial transmission of political attitudes and behavior may have been limited by generational and educational differences.

Moreover, the molding of a child, by parents and by others, may be circumscribed by his mental development. Adelson and O'Neil found impressive differences between younger and older adolescents in the consistency of their political perspectives and in their sense of community. Possibly, it is not enough for children to be exposed to mature knowledge and opinion. Their absorption of information depends on the development of cognitive capacities. This development, in turn, allows for the development of ideology.

POLITICAL IDEOLOGY

Most judges are seen, and even self-described, as possessing moderate to conservative ideologies, though there are a few liberals among them. Among black judges, however, the preponderant numbers consider themselves to be liberal. Over three fifths (63 percent) of those responding described themselves as politically liberal before they ascended to the bench. Less than a third (30 percent) described themselves as politically moderate. And a very minuscule number (3 percent) called themselves conservative, though there were 5 percent in the "other" category. This last group included the hybrids: liberal-moderate and moderate-conservative. One from this group called himself "liberal on social and economic issues... conservative on criminal justice system." Another listed his political ideology as simply "antipolitics."

A liberal in today's currency is one who advocates new approaches to societal ills; who favors extensive governmental involvement in society, especially at the federal level; and who encourages the protection of civil liberties and extensive efforts to enhance the status of blacks and the economically disadvantaged. When asked to define the term *liberal,* one judge stated: "I mean primarily that I am inclined to discard customs and practices which have been going on for some time if there is justification for doing so."

Another, from a working-class background, asserted a more explicit relationship between being black and being liberal:

> I think that if you're black, you can't be anything but liberal... It seems to me you got to believe in the philosophy that government has to help people pick themselves up by their bootstraps.

Others stated a similar theme of "progress and development in every aspect of the life of the black man."

The moderates were only half as numerous as the liberals among the black judges studied here, and they chose different ways to define their political position. For instance, one Republican replied:

> Rather than try to give you a definition, I'll give you a list of my heroes in the Republican party; people like Jacob Javits, Charles Mathias, Chuck Percy, Nelson Rockefeller, Bill Scranton.

Another Republican eschewed personalities as examples and cast his moderatism in the light of caution and a middle-of-the-road stance. He almost transformed it into a philosophy:

> Well, moderate in political terms is simply a person who will not adopt extreme philosophies... A moderate in social and philosophic terms is a

person who will always fit himself in the space of the other person before he will make a move.

A Democratic jurist ascribed her moderate designation as more a product of amalgamation than philosophy. For example, she is liberal in favoring a welfare system but conservative enough to "believe that there would be some real value to having welfare tied up with training for those who are physically able to do it."

While it would be unfair to characterize these black moderates and conservatives as being indifferent to race, most of the jurists called themselves liberal and linked their liberalism to a concern for equal rights. Indeed, race is the reason why half of the black judges are recent migrants to their jurisdictions; why they are children of the working class; and why most became interested in, and active in, politics.

Race is an elemental force in American society, but so is law. Possibly, the influence of law upon these judges will be as great as that of race.

Chapter 4
Legal Backgrounds
of Black Judges

A vocation is not merely an occupation or profession for which a person is well suited—it is an expression of personality. Members of a particular vocation possess similar personalities and similar histories of personal development. Nachman, for instance, found that lawyers (1) were noted for their verbal aggression; (2) enjoyed exercising a privileged curiosity into the lives of others; and (3) were concerned with human justice. In general, we hypothesize that members of the legal profession avoid systematic and ordered activities; understand, manipulate, and lead others through their willingness to socialize, help, enlighten, and persuade; and are ambitious, optimistic, and idealistic. Many of these personality traits are found when we examine the reasons for the black judges' choice of a legal career. Fighting for ideals of racial justice is an especially notable characteristic. As seen earlier, many respondents traced their concern for the status of black Americans to their families.

It has long been axiomatic in social science studies that the family is the single most important influence on children. Members of the family influence religion, political party affiliation, personality, and vocational interest among other things. Over a third (34 pecent) of black judges, for instance, mentioned their family as being the primary influence on their interest in becoming lawyers. Parental input was often ballasted by racial concerns. As an illustration, one Marylander chose law because he remembered that his father, a lawyer and civil rights activist,

> . . . was never satisfied . . . with the plight of black people. He felt the way to change it was through the law and through political pressure. And seeing his success, I suppose, led me to believe that was the proper and the most direct way to create change.

However, parents sometimes transmit their own personal ambitions to their children. A former Alabaman said his father wanted to be a lawyer more than anything else; and when he announced at age seven or eight that he was going to be a lawyer, both his parents encouraged him. But he qualified his statement later, saying:

> The southern black middle-class, upper middle-class, ethic is that their children should be professionals, and I suspect if my interests had been in medicine or engineering or architecture, it would have been the same thing. Anything other than a cabdriver.

Parents are not the only family members to influence vocational choice. The legal careers of brothers and uncles swayed some respondents.

Nonfamilial figures were also decisive in the black judges' selection of a career in law. The influence of such individuals is almost as extensive as that of the family. For instance, a quarter (26 percent) of these jurists stated that a friend was the primary factor in their career decision. One interviewee recalled that, when he was an undergraduate, a slightly older friend in law school convinced him that "the way a person was going to be able to cope with the problems of equal rights and equal privileges in this country was to become a lawyer."

Another 11 percent lauded a teacher as the primary influence in their choice of a legal career. One judge remembered a junior high school teacher who was "very vocal on racial matters," thereby provoking his initial fascination with law. "I thought a lawyer would be able to do more than a person in any other profession to correct the wrong."

However, almost 30 percent of the jurists cited "other" as the influence upon their career choice. These varied and provocative responses could be divided into subcategories, with the influence of nonfamily figures again notable. One set could be the dream story of a "human interest" journalist, such as the judge who became interested in law because "I worked for an aged attorney in my youth. He was blind and I read to him." Another's curiosity was provoked "as a defendant once." Still another became interested in his adolescence after reading the life story of James Weldon Johnson, the author and civil rights activist. A second group recalled their work experience as being influential: as a policeman, as a bailiff, as a laborer, as an associate of lawyers, and, for one helpful minister, when his church members had legal problems. A third collection became fascinated with law through their war and military experiences. One member of this latter group was advised to enter law school by an officer.

Lawyers have been characterized as ambitious, self-confident, and self-disciplined. A group of these black jurists appear to provide further evidence for these characterizations: they sought a career in law through no other major influence except themselves. "My own choice unaided by any primary influence," wrote one Texan. A Detroit judge said his vocational curiosity was "self-generated." And a southerner noted that he became a lawyer "by studying occupations and professions and my goals in life."

Legal counsellors are distinguished for "verbal aggression." They are talkative, even argumentative, and exhibitionistic. These personality traits were noted as factors in the career choices of some black judges. Through originally a predental student, one Detroit respondent entered law because he "enjoyed participating on the debating team." Others almost vainly noted their "speaking ability." Often, in the black American subculture, when a child is intelligent and exhibits some speaking ability, his elders will expect him to become a minister or a lawyer. This appears to have been an influence on some of the jurists. While his family wanted him to become a dentist, a Philadelphian chose law because of childhood church experiences. Adult church members thought, "I was a damn good speaker. That I was 'a good presenter,' as they say." When there were presentations to be made, he was summoned. Occasionally, members would add, "That boy's gonna be a great lawyer someday."

Some judges chose law to manipulate ("I wanted to influence others") and to gain poweer ("the need to be effective"). But many others were quite explicit in acknowledging their sensitivity to race and poverty. While the "hope to escape poverty" provoked one New Yorker, a Howard Law graduate pointed to his childhood memories of the *Scottsboro* case as the primary influence on his selection of a legal career. A New England resident was swayed by the "desire to lift the yoke of oppression from blacks." "Experiencing discrimination on the basis of race" incited a transplanted Tennessean. And another former southerner was attracted to a career in law because of the "condition of being black and poor in Virginia."

Given our previous findings that race sensitivity is an omnipresent force in the lives of black judges, these last comments are not surprising. In fact, race as the explicit rationale for selecting a career in law is probably implicit, in varying degrees, for many other black jurists as well.

Almost 40 percent of these respondents first became interested in law as a career during their youth. At the adolescent stage, there was a substantial decrease in those evincing an attraction to the law (18 percent). Yet the combined total for both stages (56 percent) far outstrips the total who exhibited a curiosity about politics (42 percent) at these stages of their lives. Since law is an inevitable product of politics, it may have led many to public activity and helped shape their attitudes on the bench.

After the period of youth, college was the next most popular phase at which the black bench was attracted to a career in law (28 percent). Those persons who became interested in a legal career through their work experience (16 percent) probably constitute the bulk of those in the "other" category.

Many of the comments made in the previous section on the primary molders of a legal undertaking serve to illuminate the reason why some chose law at the stage which they did.

UNDERGRADUATE AND LEGAL EDUCATION

Black colleges and universities have historically led an embattled existence. Neglected by most Americans and denigrated by some, they were for a long time the only avenue open to blacks in quest of a higher education. Even today, over 40 percent of black undergraduates are in black colleges. Since predominantly white schools in the north and south have only recently admitted nonwhite students in large numbers, many of these black judges were trained at black educational institutions. For example, Howard University led in both undergraduate and legal training for the respondents. Sixteen judges received their baccalaureate degrees from Howard, ten from Lincoln University, six from the University of Illinois, five from New York City College, and five from New York University. All other schools had less than five alumni on the black bench, though collectively they accounted for 77 percent of the judiciary.

It is interesting to note that while the University of Illinois, New York City College, and New York University, are cited by judges sitting in either the Chicago or New York City areas, Howard and Lincoln were cited more often by those from widely different localities. It would appear that both serve a national clientele. For blacks, Howard and Lincoln, in the past at least, might have been what Yale and Harvard were for whites—elite national universities.

As stated earlier, Howard University also trained more black judges (28) than any other law school. Besides training a quarter of the black lawyers in the United States today, Howard has also been a training ground for many civil rights activists and has been the coordinating center for numerous legal thrusts against race discrimination. Thus, it is not surprising that many Howard Law graduates recall law school as being very influential on their thinking and on their subsequent careers. One alumni recalled that he

> had such Constitutional Law and civil rights teachers as Judge James A. Cobb, James M. Nabritt (*Texas White Primary* cases), Andrew Robinson (cases involving the equalization of teachers' salaries), and perfectionists like Bernard Jefferson (now Superior Court judge in Los Angeles), and William Hastie (U.S. Court of Appeals judge).

Another noted that Howard Law School "interested me in civil rights cases and the injustices suffered by the poor." Howard Law School was the "center of meeting and preparation for most of the important civil rights cases argued in the U.S. Supreme Court," wrote one New York judge, and it provided "the opportunity for the student to participate." There were many similar comments from Howard Law graduates.

A distant second in graduating black judges is Brooklyn Law School, which was attended by fourteen judges. In turn, it was followed by New York University with seven; John Marshall of Chicago, six; Southwestern Law School in southern California, six; and Temple University in Philadelphia, five. The remaining two thirds had less than five alumni on the black bench.

Black judges are an elite group, both in relationship to the general black population as well as to the legal population. In a later effort to ascertain the relationship between race and judicial and legal socialization, this study examines the law school class rankings of, and law school influence upon, these respondents. Almost 60 percent of these black jurists were ranked in the top third of their respective law school classes. And over a third (36 percent) said that they were grouped in the middle third of their class, with a minuscule number (3 percent) in the bottom third. In addition, an even smaller number (2 percent) was uncertain of their class rank.

Law is quite often called a conservative influence because of its reliance on precedent and established procedures, among other reasons. And law school provides the initial contact with the profession. Since these respondents were predominantly liberal in their ideology, attention is now focused on the influence of law school on their thinking and subsequent careers, again in an effort to mark the relative weights of race and professional socialization upon judicial role perceptions. Slightly over half (53 percent) of these black judges felt that law school was very important in their thinking and in their subsequent careers. In contrast, a third thought it was only moderately important, and a significant number (14 percent) didn't think law school was important in the development of their legal or professional outlook. This last group constituted an unusual response since they are judges and law school is the very basis of their legal careers. As one Mid-Atlantic judge noted, "One would assume that law school would be quite instrumental in becoming a lawyer and eventually a judge." But this last group may be an extreme validation of the findings of other students of professionalization—on-the-job training that is rated far more influential than law school socialization.

As noted earlier, many of the Howard Law graduates thought law school was important because the faculty was both highly competent and very active in the civil rights movement. Some non-Howard graduates also sounded the law-as-weapon theme. An eastern judge noted that he was "highly motivated in my Constitutional Law class which in subsequent years led me to be an advocate in several landmark civil rights cases." Law school was important for another easterner because he saw "the possibilities for an egalitarian America through the sweet uses of the Constitution." "To relieve black and poor people of capitalistic oppression" was the reason given by one westerner.

But others gave quite different reasons for thinking that law school was important on their subsequent careers. A few maintained that it laid the foundation for their careers, for example, the Cleveland judge who said that law school gave him the "tools with which I could enter the mainstream of American life and be influential." For a southerner, law school was 'influential in that it taught me a new approach to problems, and convinced me that I wanted to make the legal profession my career." And for another, it was "training for disciplined thinking—made possible job and career opportunities."

For some others, law school was important because it gave them a prestigious degree; provided them with contacts; made them "feel some potential for 'success'"; and for a few, it was there that they first developed an ambition for the bench.

Law school was important for the final group of black judges because it furnished insight into the operations of the political system and showed the necessity for political activity. One New Yorker intoned that law school "made me more aware of the hypocrisy basic to the governmental structure of this country." "The need for Negroes to become involved in politics" became apparent to an Ohio judge while in law school. And for another, it "broadened by conceptions of the problems of society." Rationalizations such as these appear to be restatements of the concern for race that characterized the first group.

The proposition that law, and consequently law school, is a conservative force could not be easily substantiated by these findings. Too many judges said that law school gave them the tools by which to fight racism and classism, though many gave completely different reasons. The more likely proposition would be that law school confirmed each respondent's previous inclination. As one Los Angeles judge noted, "Many of my fundamental beliefs were confirmed in rules of law or in ideas of my instructors." When asked whether law school and legal training make him conservative, one personally interviewed easterner replied,

> Oh no. Breaking out of past patterns is something which I think I have always had a tendency toward wanting to do. If law school did anything, I suppose it helped to sharpen by ability to do this.

Thus, law school was not perceived as a conservative socializing agent by black judges. It merely confirmed their previous inclinations. One of their major concerns was race, and law school provided many with an instrument by which to lessen discrimination against blacks.

PREBENCH CAREER

If every man is the sum of his experiences, then his job experience must be considered an integral part of the man. An adult probably spends as much time at his job as he spends in waking hours with his family. There are many forces and influences impinging upon and shaping the outlooks of each individual. To get a greater knowledge of the individual, his job background must be examined, especially since on-the-job training has been rated so highly as a socializing agent. In this section, the prebench careers of black judges are scrutinized.

As with law school training, the prebench backgrounds are diverse, though a plurality of them were concentrated in private practice. Almost two thirds of the judges were private practitioners before ascendsng to the bench. However, to lump them into private practice would perhaps underemphasize the diversity of their job experiences. Others have noted the opportunities that a lawyer has for lateral entry in and out of public and private jobs, and these black judges when practicing attorneys, seem to have availed themselves of these opportunities. While 64 percent had made a career of private practice, only 38 percent entered into it directly from law school, and only slightly more (44 percent) were still in it immediately before going on the bench.

The difficulties black lawyers encounter in establishing their practice have been noted in the past. Oftentimes, they take full-time positions in other fields and practice law in their spare time. They then build a clientele or kitty before going into law on a full-time basis. Something comparable seems to have happened with some of these judges, though overall they may have been a bit luckier than most black lawyers. Almost 40 percent went immediately into private practice after law school; another 17 percent were serving clerkships, heading for quite respectable legal careers. But 14 percent were in the civil service, many with that legendary citadel of black employment, the federal post office; and another 13 percent were doing jobs listed as "other," including factory work, menial work, defense construction, and military service. Eventually this last sizable chunk of respondents partially established themselves; only 7 percent of the total remain in the civil service and other occupations under the primary career job category.

One eastern judge recalled his experience of working immediately after law school and before establishing himself in practice:

> While working as a housing inspector, I passed the bar examinations. I continued working for a while...After I passed the bar I did a little moonlighting practice...taking a little time off whenever I could from the job. See, at the time I had two young children to support.

This seems to be the story for many of those who did not go immediately into private practice; they did not have the wherewithal or contacts to establish a legal practice.

Another pattern in the career development of these judges was government service including the military. One jurist explains the start of his legal career,

> I passed the bar during 1942...But at the time, the war was going on and I had a government job, so I remained in the government...After I went into the Army and came out...I went back to the government job for about a year and then I went into private practice.

A stint in the military was not too unusual; some of the respondents followed this route before establishing their practice.

Clerkships accounted for a good proportion of those in the "first-job" category (over 17 percent), and of those personally interviewed, three started their legal careers in this position. One was required by state law to clerk for a lawyer with a long-standing practice before being certified by the state. Another got a position as clerk for a federal judge immediately after law school. And finally, there is the case of the judge who was refused a position in a large white firm because of his race. Through the aid of a black politician, he was hired by the firm of a local politico. The lawyer

> gave me a job as his law assistant, call it a clerk if you want to. Doing all the hard work in the office, doing all the legal thinking in the office. While he goes to court and does the case, I'm sitting on my rear end in that office.

Needless to say, this frustrated barrister soon left that firm and hung out his own shingle.

Of those judges who were interviewed, the results of their efforts to establish a practice were somewhat mixed, with most having a relatively easy time. One Republican used his party connections to enhance and facilitate his legal practice; "The black leadership of that party were friends of mine through social relationships. So it was just a step for me to go from lawyer to politics." He had no difficulty ("none whatever") in establishing himself.

A Democrat in the same city reports, "From the day (my partner) and I opened our office, we had one problem—that was finding time to turn out the work." Another Democrat reported that he had no difficulty in getting established twenty-five years ago. In fact, he opened his law office before he even graduated from law school. "I think my first year, I made about thirty-one hundred dollars, which I didn't think was bad...(and) all I wanted to do in those days was play pinochle and drink Pepsi-Cola. I didn't need a lot of money."

One judge in this small interview sample who reported having trouble getting established had problems for a short period of time. "Oh, I had a hard time for the first six months," he said, "Negroes didn't believe in Negro lawyers in those days (1924). I had a tough time." But he was the only one of those personally interviewed to characterize his early practice in such harsh terms. It is possible that the experiences of these particular judges were not representative of all black judges nor for all black lawyers, since previous studies clearly conclude that many black attorneys have difficulty establishing their law practice.

The prosecutor's office is often thought to be a stepping stone to judicial and political positions. The findings in this study help to substantiate this belief. Less than 10 percent of these judges had their first job in the district attorney's office, but 17 percent listed it as their career job. And, most telling, over a fifth (23 percent) of them worked in that office as their last job before going on the bench.

This phenomenon of advancement is even greater in the category of "Public

Positions." The category refers to nonprosecutorial, appointive positions, usually second- and third-ranking offices in state and municipal bureaucracies. Though slightly less than 3 percent secured such a position as their first job, three times that number (9 percent) describe that position as their primary career job. An even more substantial number, 19 percent, held such a position as their last before going on the bench. From these data, it would appear that visibility and being in the right place are helpful in being tapped for a judgeship.

One judge, not politically active but well placed, visible, and able, recalled the experience of moving from the district attorney's office:

> Both the district attorney...and the attorney general...urged me to become a judge. The district attorney persuaded the county chairman to recommend me. The attorney general persuaded the governor to appoint me. I subsequently ran and won a ten-year term.

Another judge, among those interviewed, also went from the office of the prosecutor to a judicial position. But he ascended differently than most; he was elected to his bench. While in the prosecutor's office, he saw not only the enormous power that judges possess but also the dual standards of justice being applied. He documented this discriminatory treatment both in the prosecutor's office and on the bench, and subsequently published it in a local newspaper. Thus, he had an audience when he announced his candidacy for the judiciary. His campaign stance was "being a person who was sensitive enough to see that change was desired and with enough courage to try to create that change." He relied on no organizations, political or otherwise, black or otherwise. "I felt that power was in the people as opposed to political organization," so he relied upon the press to disseminate his views and the public to coalesce around his candidacy.

Henderson and Sinclair, in their study of Texas judges, found both the prosecutor's office and a high position in a public bureaucracy to be salient features of prebench careers; this was especially true for trial court judges in their first and last job before ascending the bench. This study of black judges finds the same pattern, but not as overwhelmingly. Almost three fourths of the Texas trial judges studied made their initial entry into legal careers with positions in the prosecutor's office or that of public bureaucracies; while only 13 percent of these black judges did so. Approximately two thirds of the Texas trail court judges held such positions immediately before going on the bench; whereas slightly over 40 percent of the black jurists held such positions. This latter contrast reflects not only the growing employment of blacks in these areas but also represents a closing of the gap between these blacks and the Texans who moved from there to the bench. If the Texas findings are any indication, public positions are almost ideal stations for moving up to judgeships, and more blacks seem to be attaining these ideal launching places. The ratio of black judges who made their initial career entry in these positions to those employed there as a last post is more than 1 to 3, which probably indicates a greater sensitivity on the part of the employing agents. In other words, the difference may represent an easing of discrimination against black lawyers.

In his study of black professionals conducted in the late 1940s Edwards found that the lawyer was the notable exception to the pattern of entering a professional occupation following college training. Less than a third of the lawyers entered their profession, Edwards observed; whereas two thirds of the judges here went into professional occupations. Only 12 percent of the lawyers in Edwards's study went into the full-time practice of law following completion of the bar examination, while almost 60 percent continued with some other type of employment, though a third did open part-time law offices. By contrast, almost 40 percent of these respondents began their law career in full-time private practice. Another quarter of the total either clerked or found jobs in the public sector. Thus the career development of the black lawyer may be changing. In any case, more career studies are necessary of both lawyers and judges, blacks and whites.

Further scrutiny of the prebench legal work history of black jurists indicates, on the other hand, that they suffered fates comparable to nonblack minority attorneys. In the last three quarters of this century, a stratified bar has emerged in urban America. At the lower levels, ethnic solo practitioners from working-class backgrounds, after initial trouble establishing their practice, engage in general legal problem solving; procure clients from neighborhood associations and local political contacts; and participate in such low-paying trial work as criminal law, personal injury, divorce, and collections. Our respondents are similar to these white ethnic attorneys.

Since 80 percent of northern blacks reside in central cities, it is not surprising to find that 96 percent of these black judges had maintained legal practices in urban areas. A rural clientele engaged 2 percent; a like number combined a city-country practice. Few blacks are in the suburbs and a lone respondent had worked there. Over 60 percent of the jurists had been solo practitioners, while only a third had been affiliated with law firms and 4 percent had done both. As practicing attorneys, the respondents catered to fellow blacks. Over four fifths had a mostly black clientele, while a tenth counseled mostly whites. Their legal specialty appears to have been general problem solving, often in court. Three out of four had operated at the trial level, representing both plaintiffs and defendants in civil and criminal cases. Moreover, judges are generally underpaid compared to other legal professionals, yet only a fifth of black jurists suffered a decrease in income after donning their robes. Though not among the high-salaried corporate counsels of the legal profession, our respondents nevertheless enjoyed comfortable incomes before coming on the bench.

In summary, while family and peers had an impact on the career choice of black judges, race was a factor (1) in their legal education and socialization; and

(2) in their career patterns and law practices. A concern for the advancement of black Americans has characterized almost every aspect of the lives of Afro-American jurists. Professional role, which should presumably have surfaced in this examination of their legal careers, was notable for its absence. However, it may appear in their recruitment to the judiciary.

Chapter 5
Recruitment of Black Judges

The American political system is based upon the rule of law, at least in principle. Since judges interpret the law, they are among the most powerful actors in the society. They have the authority to fix bail, convict, sentence, and award damages. Judicial positions are highly sought prizes because of their power and prestige and long tenure. Yet not much is known about how or when lawyers become interested in ascending to the judiciary. While slightly more is known about judicial recruitment, there is still need for further research. Judicial interest and recruitment are the focus of this chapter. Both are scrutinized for their possible impact on the attitudes of black judges.

In contrast to political socialization and legal ambition, it would appear that the urge for a judgeship does not begin early, at least not for black judges. Only 6 percent had been infected with a yearning for a judicial post by the time they graduated from college, with an additional 3 percent acquiring the yen in law school. For nine out of ten of the members of the black bench, the desire came during their practice of law.

And again, unlike the response seen on political and legal interest, neither the family nor teacher is a significant influence on the itch for the bench. Only 5 percent of the subjects noted the family as a factor; their teachers were cited by only 1 percent. However, while friends were pointed to in almost a fifth (19 percent) of the cases, considerably more than half of the black bench (56 percent) emphasized thir law practice as the source of their wish to ascend to a judgeship. The category of "other" acounted for almost a fifth (19 percent) of the respondents. One judge ascribed his judicial ambition to his lawyer-father's wish to have his son become a justice of the United States Supreme Court. This is probably typical of those who stressed the family influence. But in the "other" category, a variety of reasons is cited. Some judges said that their thoughts about the judiciary were provoked by the opportunity to be appointed. Others cited political activity as the primary influence. A few were urged to seek a judicial position by other persons, for instance, members of the community or fellow black lawyers or the district attorney. Personal ambition was the precipitating factors for some others.

Racial considerations were influential factors on the judicial ambition of some of these black jurists. One lawyer became interested in the judiciary because of the "necessity for blacks to be elected." Another noted his interest "when as a boy we complained of no black judges." Yet another cited his "own desire and will to prove that a black lawyer could be the best judge on the bench." Finally, one Far West judge tersely wrote "anger" as his primary influence. Thus for some black judges, race is never far from their consciousness, even when it relates to judicial ambition.

Among those claiming law practice as the primary influence, one eastern judge recounted his escalating ambition for the bench:

> When you go to law school, in the back of your mind, you say, "gee, I would like to be a judge... Before law school, I think my principal aim was to go to law school and become a lawyer. After you reach that stage then you go to the next one... After practicing in the court, you have respect for that person who sits on the bench and who makes these decisions... This was a challenge (to make those decisions); you're a lawyer, so you want to go up.

When asked to be more specific about what attracted him to the judiciary, he replied, "I guess it was more or less the respect, the power" of the position.

A politically active Republican in the East explained his judicial interest as flowing from a lack of opportunity for influence in partisan politics.

> I went on the bench for one reason and one reason only: I've had a deep and abiding concern all my life about the political and legal health, about the community in which I live... I began to see that in those (party) positions there was little opportunity, as the political situation... then existed, of affecting the changes and the health of the community through that political process... Thus, I turned to my second love, the law, which is an equal love... I concluded that I could most affect it (the legal health of the community) from the bench as opposed to private practice. Some people thought I was qualified to go on the bench. I do too; I am not a modest person. If good people won't take judicial positions, then they have no standing to complain when the hacks get positions.

Of course, it would be simplistic to assume that the judicial interest for any of these judges is based upon one factor alone. Rather it appears to be based upon a combination of factors: ambition, power, prestige, the ability to affect change—*a la* activists in political parties. One judge who had long nurtured judicial ambitions recalls the initial interest being planted by his father, a lawyer, who "reflected his desire and his belief that I would become a member of the Supreme Court of the United States. That has always stuck with me and it played some role, I would suppose, in my filing for the (bench), because I knew the impact it would have on him." This judge also alludes to power and racial discrimination as factors awakening his interest in becoming a judge:

> As a prosecutor, appearing before various members of the bench on a daily basis, again I recognized what a tremendous amount of control they had over the citizenry. . . . The other thing was of course the way I was treated by the bench in certain circumstances, namely, my being suspended for suggesting dual standards of justice existed. . .

Another judge highlights how he became interested in the judiciary along with why he accepted the position:

> During my youth. . . I was planning to become a lawyer, but it never occurred to me to be a judge. . . But I think it's an ambition most lawyers acquire. . . To a lawyer who has been practicing law for many years, being a judge is a classic continuation (of the profession). But perhaps more importantly. . . I feel a judge is sometimes in a better position to correct a lot of problems than people in other areas. . .

Since so many of these black judges chose law practice as the stage at which they develop interest in a judicial position, it is plausible to conclude that judgeships were not visible enough during their childhood for them to dream of reaching this pinnacle of power and prestige. As one of the judges indicated, it was escalating ambition: from law school; to law practice; to involvement in public affairs, especially civil rights; and then to the judiciary.

While the family may have been the principal agent for the child's interest in law as a profession, ambition for the bench usually came as a result of later, specific professional experiences. The influences and periods of initial judicial ambition of black judges are so similar that they would appear to have little affect on variations in role perceptions.

JUDICIAL RECRUITMENT

Elections provide the mechanism for choosing public officeholders in a democratic nation. The citizenry is asked to choose from among many candidates the persons it wishes to lead the different branches of government.

Elections decide winners and losers, and help to determine the course of governmental action. Through voting, the people legitimize their leaders. But there is evidence that the voter is being shortchanged; *de jure* elective offices are becoming de facto appointive ones. For instance, Prewitt found that nearly a fourth of the city councilmen he studied were appointed to their elective nonpartisan positions.

The American judiciary has not operated on the elective principle as extensively as the other branches of government. For example, the federal judiciary has always been an appointive one, and numerous state governments have followed this lead. Yet other jurisdictions have mandated that the electorate should choose its judges. Today, with blacks heavily concentrated in urban areas, some black judges have argued that an elective bench should be maintained. Their reasoning follows classic democratic theory: the government should reflect the desires of its citizens. More particularly, elected black judges will be more sensitive to black needs. The remainder of this chapter has a two-part focus: (1) to discover how black judges were recruited to the judiciary; and (2) to isolate those factors (racial, professional, and others) they thought important in their selection.

Slightly over a quarter (26 percent) of the respondents were presiding over partisan elective tribunals, while an additional 29 percent sat on nonpartisan elective ones. Yet, though 55 percent of the judgeships were listed as elective, less than a quarter (23 percent) of the black bench initially received their posts on the basis of such direct voter sentiment. In other words, over three quarters (77 percent) of Afro-American jurists were appointed to the judiciary, though only 45 percent were officially designated as such including the 5 percent specified under the Missouri Plan. In short, a great number, a sum of fifty-nine, came to elective benches through appointment.

This is not surprising. Though many localities stipulate that judges be elected, these relatively low-visibility public officers are often chosen without voter approval. Henderson and Sinclair found that half of the elective judgeships in Texas were occupied by appointees. Ish discovered the same phenomenon in California. This extensive use of executive designation is abetted by a host of institutional factors. The proscription of the judicial role precludes a discussion of issues in court elections that in turn hinders high stimulus contests and lessens voter interest. Moreover, reform movements have removed partisan labels, rearranged ballot formats, and changed election schedules. All of these variables have diminished voter turnout and made judgeships attractive awards to the party faithful.

In a personal interview, one of our respondents noted that he was the first judge in fifteen years initially elected to his wholy elective court. This is an apt comment on how valuable these judgeships are as patronage plums; how much power they give the appointing office; and how pervasive the appointment process operates. Such appointments are made when the previous judge dies or resigns from the bench, and they allow the appointing executive, quite often the governor, to repay his political debts while leving his mark and his men on the judiciary. Judicial positions are not the most visible of offices, and once a judge is on the bench, it is almost his to keep. In Texas, for example, the rate of judicial turnover was found to be less than 5 percent a year.

As widespread as the appointment process is, it is more prevalent for elective nonpartisan judgeships than for elective partisan ones. For example, only a quarter of black judges on elective nonpartisan benches were initially elected to their position, but three fifths of those sitting on elective partisan tribunals were first given their mandate by the voters. Elective nonpartisan judgeships have effectively become appointive ones.

In an effort to illuminate the factors that were instrumental in their ascent to the bench, these judges were given a list of influences and were asked to indicate those that were important. Thus, a check was considered to be an affirmative response, while a "no" or a blank was treated as a negative answer. With this system, each factor will have a total of 185 responses, the number of questionnaires received. The affirmative answers are the more significant ones since they are based upon the active participation of the respondents. This discussion will isolate the factors that influence elective versus appointive judicial selection. In addition, it will help pinpoint the influences of race and professionalism on the recruitment of members of the black bench.

Political party affiliation has previously been found to be the most important factor in judicial elections, especially partisan ones. But in judicial appointments, bar associations have been more important than party, though both are present. When elective judgeships become in effect appointive ones, the politics shifts from the electorate to the appointing officer. The salient factors then become those that are characteristic of the appointive bench. Thus, it is not surprising to see these mostly appointed black judges choose professional standing (68 percent), political party (56 percent), and friends (40 percent), as the most outstanding major influences in their judicial ascent. All other components were less frequently noted, though a possibly significant 30 percent tabbed black voters as a factor in their move to the bench. While a tenth pointed to the press, 14 percent checked civil rights groups, and 16 percent marked "other."

The politics of the appointing officer is a complex process involving numerous factors. Some of our respondents noted the interplay of these factors. One Pennsylvania judge who was appointed to an elective seat "sought support of political and community leaders and bar associations." A Chicagoan "made application through his bar association and with my political party." His personal campaign led him to see "my ward committeeman and the president of the local bar assocation."

One Lower Atlantic jurist, in recalling his rise through his appointment from a part-time judge to a magistrate to a judge of an elective bench, evokes all three major factors. His recollection graphically illustrates the complex politics of the appointing officer. A friend and former law partner appointed him to a part-time position, telling him, "You can pick up yourself a few extra dollars." After moving to the status of magistrate, he recalled, an elective judgeship opened up.

> But we could not get a black lawyer on the bar list to be recommended for judge, except one...who was a Republican. And they called me up just before the deadline and said, 'Bob, you better put your name in or we won't have a black judge.'...They felt (the governor) would not want a Republican, and then he could say to us, 'Look, I can't appoint a black; I only appoint Democrats.' And sure enough, I got on the list, and he wouldn't appoint not one Republican on that bench, out of fourteen judges.

After having been offered the position, he was pressured by other black lawyers to accept. "Bob, you can't think of yourself. You've got to make a way for your people, and unless we have a black judge, we go backward." So he accepted.

While these three examples explain the politics of the appointing officer, other comments further isolate the importance of individual factors upon particular paths of bench recruitment. Professional standing was cited most often, and was especially notable in the appointment process. Almost three quarters (72 percent) of black jurists who were initially appointed to their benches said that professional standing was important, while slightly more than half (54 percent) of those initially elected indicated that it was an important recruitment factor. One appointed judge wrote that he was recommended "by the senior judge of the court who was familiar with my abilities." A midwesterner stated that "a fellow college classmate of mine who was a judge believed that I would make a good judge and was instrumental in my appointment." One respondent almost bragged that he "was asked by the bar association" to accept an appointment.

Political party affiliation is most striking for its influence in elective politics, especially partisan ones. For instance, almost nine tenths (87 percent) of black judges on elective partisan benches felt that political party affiliation was important in their judicial recruitment, while slightly more than half (54 percent) on elective nonpartisan and less than two fifths (38 percent) on appointive tribunals felt the same. Moreover, this pattern continues for initial entry: eight tenths (81 percent) of those who first received their judgeships in an election thought that political party affiliation was an important influence on their recruitment, though less than half (48 percent) of the initially appointed stated as much.

The comments of respondents provide further testimony to the well-documented influence of the party, even for appointed judges. For instance, while noting his irregular route to the bench, one Democratic party faithful "never was concerned that if I made my position known that it wouldn't be honored...I'm on the Democratic Central Committee, and (it) is endorsing the Democrats in power." On the other side, an Ohio Republican "indicated I would be available and made the same known to the Republican Central Committee." Some other Republicans provide even more telling testimony of the influence of party on judicial recruitment. They were "sacrificial lambs," campaigning valiantly for their party but losing. One GOP member recalled that "I ran for election at the request of the party against an opponent we all knew I could not defeat." His reward was a judgeship. Finally, one epigrammatic Chicagoan penned that a "career in politics automatically leads to opportunity."

Judgeships are among the few remaining patronage plums available to big city political organizations, and it is noteworthy that many elected respondents citing the party factor come from highly urbanized areas, especially New York and Chicago. While some judges in these cities did not rely upon their party service for entree into the judge's chambers, many did. One New Yorker "developed and advanced step-by-step in the local Democratic organization." Thus, it appears that political parties in densely populated areas serve more as a filter for court positions than they do in less populated, less urbanized localities. In the large, stratified cities, the party structures the judicial recruitment process.

After professional standing and political party, the most frequently noted influence on judicial recruitment was friendship. The appointive-elective schism noted before on more popular recruitment influences continues here, but is less noticeable. Friends were more important for judges who were initially appointed (41 percent) than for those initially elected (35 percent). Interestingly, judges on elective nonpartisan courts were more likely to say that friends were important (48 percent) than either appointive (37 percent) or elective partisan (34 percent) incumbents. Since elective nonpartisan judgeships have become in effect appointive ones, political friends are especially important. One appointed westerner "told the governor who was a friend, of my interest if there were a vacancy on the bench." But others worked more indirectly. For example, one told "a powerful politically active law friend," while a Texan "made my friends in the (state) senate aware of my interest."

The black judges' citation of professional standing, political party, and friendship, as important judicial recruitment factors confirms the operation of the politics of the appointing officer. The saliency of this process is underscored by the degree to which appointments have limited the power of electors: two fifths of black judges on officially elective partisan courts and, even more telling, three quarters of those on officially elective nonpartisan benches, did not receive their initial mandate from the voters.

The extensiveness of appointments to fill elective positions has led one observer to formulate rationales for such behavior. Prewitt thinks such appointments serve three strategic purposes: (1) insuring like-minded successors; (2) co-opting spokesmen from dissident groups; and (3) building a coalition. These strategies are not necessarily mutually exclusive; for instance, co-opting a dissident may also help build a coalition. Even so, some examples of each purpose can be found in the comments of black judges. That of selecting like-minded successors can be ascertained from the remarks of a political moderate (sitting on an elective bench) who, as an assistant prosecutor, was urged by the district attorney and the state attorney general to become a judge. "The attorney general persuaded the governor to appoint me...I was not politically active; in fact (I) did not know my committeeman nor ward leader."

The strategy of co-opting dissidents is shown by the appointment of a Pennsylvanian to an elective judgeship, after he had fought his city's political establishment for over thirty years.

Using appointments to build coalitions is a widely used strategy, and a number of black judges testified to that effect. For instance, for one upstate New Yorker, "various political acquaintances started to demand a black judge and made a political deal with the man running for mayor." A New York City respondent, "backed the right candidate and was asked to fill a vacancy."

The electoral process has been aborted in the appointment of blacks to elective judgeships. Less than a quarter of our subjects were initially elected to their benches. Yet there is evidence that some of the elections are farces. Many Chicagoans and some New Yorkers spoke of being "slated by Democratic party to run as judge." In strong one-party municipalities, judicial candidates are selected at the political clubhouse. The effective selection is not done by public officials or by voters. Indeed, the voters are given the "free choice" of confirming the selection, abstaining, or pulling the lever for a loser, usually a Republican.

All of these revelations must be distressing to those who advocate that the black citizenry should elect its judges. Black voters are slighted as an influence in the selection of Afro-American judges; further proof that black voters are not choosing black judicial representatives. For example, less than 30 percent of the respondents cited black electors as an important factor in their judicial recruitment, though this corresponds rather closely to the quarter who were initially elected to their judicial posts. But even here the elective-appointive division continues. Judges who were initially elected are more likely to state that black voters were important (42 percent) than those who were initially appointed (26 percent). This may provide some slight encouragement to those black interest-group democrats who advocate using black voters to increase the racial sensitivity of the judiciary, especially when this division is found in responses about the influence of civil rights groups. While civil rights groups were said to be influential in judicial recruitment by less than 15 percent of these respondents, those jurists who were initially elected are twice as likely to note that civil rights groups were important as those who were initially appointed to the bench (23 percent versus 11 percent, respectively). Moreover, almost 40 percent answered, to another question, that black interest groups helped them get on the bench. These groups were ministerial alliances, local black bar associations, Jaycees, and the like.

Nevertheless, these Afro-American judges acknowledge that black voters, civil rights groups, and black interest groups, were less influential than other factors in their rise to the bench. They did indicate, however, that their race was very influential in their recruitment. In answer to the pointed question as to whether their race was an important aid, almost four fifths (78 percent) of the respondents answered affirmatively, while a fifth replied negatively. An Illinois respondent confessed, "I was appointed because I was black. There is no need to try to twist it."

The differences between elective and appointive recruitment continues on the explicit question of race but has undergone a curious reversal. As seen earlier, elected black judges more often cited racial factors (black voters and civil rights groups) as important in their selection than did their appointed brethren. Yet when asked if race itself was an important recruitment factor, appointed respondents were more likely (75 percent) than elected ones (67 percent) to answer affirmatively. While the difference is not great, the reversal raises the possibility that the appointing officer may have used his powers to insure like-minded successors on the bench, to co-opt dissidents, or to build coalitions, especially since the increase in black judges follows the increase in black political agitation.

A further indication of the importance of race may be seen when examining those black judges who were initially elected to their benches. Those elective nonpartisan contests were more likely (79 percent) to state that race was important than respondents who won their positions in elective partisan campaigns (64 percent). In the absence of political party designations, race assumes greater saliency for the voter.

Three of the eleven personally interviewed judges thought that their race was not an important help in their judicial ascent. One Democrat from the Mid-Atlantic recalled that "race might have been one of the detractors in (my) getting on the bench." First appointed in the early 1960s, he indicated that he might have gone on sooner if he had not been black.

Another appointee who answered negatively, a Republican from the Upper-Atlantic region, eventually qualified his answer during the interview:

> I think I would have gotten on the bench. I don't think that the fact that I was black was as important as the service that I had given to the party. . . I think the primary consideration with me was the fact that I was a black who had served, you understand, not simply that I was black, but I was a black who had served the party. . . (Race) was an important part but not the most important. Okay?

The third negative response to the importance of race was a judge who was initially appointed to an elective position, who then ran for a full term. Upon reflection, however, she admitted that race "probably had something to do with it," since she was appointed to replace a black incumbent. Nevertheless, when she campaigned for election, race did not play a part. "Nobody seemed to bother about it and I didn't bother about. I didn't run as a black; I didn't run as a white; I ran as the best person for the judgeship." Thus, upon further examination, two of the three negative answers indicated that race was a positive influence.

Even so, their ambivalent attitude was a minority view. The remaining eight judges who were personally interviewed all acknowledge that their race was important in their ascent to the bench. For those who were initially appointed to the bench, their appointment was a latter-day replay of classical urban politics, the play for the ethnic vote. One senior judge noted that race

> was important because the party that wanted me... the Democratic party, wanted to make a big hit with the black people. And the black people were growing more and more then.

Another judge stated that

> when you're living in a community... that's ethnically oriented, you have to recognize there's always an effort to try and placate all elements of the particular community. And we have a large black vote... in this city.

And he admitted that his appointment was an effort to "throw out something for the black community," though his judgeship was all the group had gotten so far. And another saw his appointment as part of a quid pro quo, in return for black support during the governor's bid for office.

Needless to say, the two judges who were initially elected to their judgeships, a relatively rare feat for either blacks or whites, were even more forthright in acknowledging the importance of their race. One of them recalled that the only groundwork for his candidacy was to "create an interest in the black public generally," and his preliminary exploits of documenting discrimination in the local criminal justice system had already whetted the interest of the black community.

In summary, elections, to the limited degree to which they operate in the judiciary, appear to have been generally aborted in the recruitment of black judges. Black voters were perceived as not nearly as influential as professional standing, political party, and friendship; these are factors commonly associated with the politics of the appointing officer. Professional standing and friends were important factors for the appointed black judges; political party and, to a lesser extent, black voters were cited by elected ones. However, race was found to be an important help for the great majority of respondents, both appointed and elected, though the other factors, especially professional standing, may have mediated racial influence to the extent that it may affect the role perceptions of the black bench.

The selection of blacks through appointments was found to be comparable to other state and local judges and even to nonjudicial officeholders. Nevertheless, the extensive appointment of black jurists raises the question of whether the appointing officers may be using their powers to build a coalition, on one hand, by appointing moderate blacks, on the other. Given the long-running American practice of using individual blacks as symbols and role models, this suspicion cannot be lightly disregarded. For example, a Nixon appointee, a Republican moderate, recollected being discreetly approached by administration officials questioning his actions on the bench. His example notwithstanding, the appointment process for the federal judiciary is notable for weeding out extremists and mavericks as well as incompetents. The same results may have occurred in the sifting of blacks for the judiciary at both federal and state levels, even though such uses of the appointment powers are not peculiarly confined to race. The affects of elections versus appointment on the thoughts of black judges will be studied after we investigate their civil rights activity.

Chapter 6
Civil Rights Activity of Black Judges

The struggle for the equality of black people in this country has been a long and varied one. Of the many techniques used in this struggle, one of the most successful and durable has been litigation in the courts of America, where many of the struggle's biggest headlines have been made. Until blacks marched *en masse* in the streets to inaugurate the 1960s, litigation was the predominant thrust in the struggle to equalize black and white status, and had been for almost half a century. Adjudication is a long and costly process. Since these black judges were once practicing attorneys, an examination of their civil rights activity can provide an easily accessible indication of the scope and degree of their race consciousness. Given the influence of race on their socialization and judicial recruitment, a differentiation of civil rights activity may help to refine the influence of race on judicial role perceptions.

One civil rights activist, Judge Robert Carter, has stated that most black lawyers were not significantly involved in the civil rights movement. But these black judges indicate that they, when practicing attorneys, were active in civil rights. Two fifths of these respondents classified themselves as very active, while almost half (47 percent) stated that they were moderately active. The remaining judges described themselves as not at all active. This finding seemingly refutes Carter's assertion, but it may be that these jurists were the most active of the black lawyers. Possibly, they were the ones with the intelligence, the hustle, the connections, and the concern who eventually parlayed their many attributes into a judge's robe.

The extent of the civil rights activism of these black jurists can be refined even further. Almost 90 percent of the respondents listed themselves as members of some civil rights organization. Combining explicitly negative responses and blank responses, the percentage claiming no civil rights membership (13 percent) very closely approximates those who claimed no civil rights activity whatever (12.6 percent).

Equally significant, these respondents were not merely members but active ones. They were contributors (75 percent) and workers (65 percent), which included picketing and stuffing envelopes. And most significant, almost half (47 percent) claimed to have been officers in one or more of these organizations. From this data, it would appear that the fight for racial equality was highly important to these black judges.

While facts thus far exposited about these respondents would indicate that they were moving to reshape the American polity, such indications may be deceptive. Though these jurists were clustered at the left or liberal end of the sociopolitical spectrum, they would be more accurately characterized as reformers than as revolutionaries. This characterization can be most easily, though only partially, substantiated by examining the civil rights organizations with which they were affiliated. In an almost uncanny coincidence, those claiming membership in the National Association for the Advancement of Colored People (NAACP) — 86 percent — nearly equals those claiming membership in some civil rights organization — 87 percent. While civil rights activity and the NAACP may by synonymous, this coincidence probably reflects the NAACP's emphasis on litigation. Half of the respondents claimed membership in the Urban League, with less than 10 percent noting membership in any other organization. Though almost 20 percent cited membership in "other" civil rights groups, often ones based in their local communities, nationally known associations such as the Congress of Racial Equality (10 percent), the Southern Christian leadership Conference (7 percent), and the Student Nonviolent Coordinating Committee (3 percent), found very few adherents among these ebon jurists.

Both the NAACP and the Urban League were the most conservative of the better-known civil rights groups. Clark, a well-known civil rights activist, has written that these two most prominent civil rights organizations "shared a basic assumption that major changes in the status of the Negro could be obtained within the framework of the American democratic system." The primary focus of the NAACP was on political and legal power, while simultaneously seeking to reach the conscience of white Americas through propaganda. The Urban League, on the other hand, emphasized and negotiated with the power centers—economic, industrial, and governmental—of American society. Both organizations were educational groups seeking to appeal to reason through research, dissemination of information, consultation, persuasion, and negotiation with economic and political leaders. The Urban League provided, as Young has noted, "a unique machinery for effective cooperation between white and Negro citizens to avoid social misunderstanding and strife." This same cooperative, interracial, melioristic thinking characterized the NAACP, though it emphasized litigation and legislaiton. Both organizations "took literally the ideology and promises of the system and shared unquestioningly American optimism."

While these two organizations had a significant number of adherents among black judges, the lesser-known, younger, and more militant civil rights groups had a very minuscule following. Slightly less than 10 percent of these respondents claimed membership in the Congress of Racial Equality (CORE), with the Southern Christian Leadership Conference (SCLC) and the Student Nonviolent Coordinating Committee (SNCC) having even less than that.

These three more militant organizations sought to appeal to morality through direct personal confrontation and the dramatization of the effects of discrimination. They appealed to the tacit bystanders while engaging the enforcers of segregation head-to-head. Their primary target was discrimination in public accommodations, and their favorite tactic was the sit-in. In fact, CORE has seemingly specialized in this method of protest. Since its founding in 1942, one of CORE's basic tenets was that law alone could not win the war against segregation.

Although CORE's "rather constricted, dedicated, almost cultlike group of racial protesters" utilized direct confrontation for many years, this tactic reached a crescendo in the late 1950s and 1960s, when it was fully imported into the South and successfully used by SCLC and SNCC. All three organizations impatiently pressed for full and immediate equality for blacks. The persuading, propagandizing, and negotiating so characteristic of the NAACP and the Urban League were not as attractive to the followers of the more militant organizations.

As shown through their civil rights activity, these black judges have indicated a moderate to high concern for racial equality, even if most restricted their activity to the more conservative organizations. A concern for civil rights is not the exclusive province of any group of these jurists. They were black and had to confront the cold realities of discrimination and inequality as did their less fortunate brethren.

In previous chapters, we saw that racial discrimination was the precipitating factor in the interest and activity of these black jurists in politics as well as interest in law. We now turn to personal interviews to flesh out the duration and degree of this concern for civil rights.

For some of these black judges, interest in black equality was planted by parents and teachers in secondary school and in college. One rather senior judge related the heretofore undisclosed fact that his father had been born a slave. One Philadelphia respondent stated that he had "always been interested in civil rights. I held a junior membership in the NAACP years and years ago."

One Mid-Atlantic judge recalled the seeds of his interest as well as of his activity:

> . . . not only my mother, but I had some good teachers that hopped on this race thing. But getting into CORE was interesting. . . This was 1955 or '56 or thereabouts. I was involved in a couple of civic organizations. There was

this white fellow...also a member of these civic organizations...One night, I was passing the corner...and I saw this group of people picketing; all the restaurants were segregated then. And this fellow...I saw him among the pickets. And I asked myself a question here: "this white fellow was out picketing for civil rights; why shouldn't I be picketing?" And I talked to him the next time I saw him. I asked him how I could get involved.

But others did not wait this long to become involved. For instance, another judge recounted his initial activity as a summer recreational worker in his hometown where he noticed a "vast difference" in playground facilities for blacks and whites.

I called newspaper reporters to come out and look...and to compare our facilities with what the white playgrounds had. I believe that was...my first act that I have ever performed as far as civil rights. That was during high school.

And his activity continued in college where he joined the NAACP and CORE to fight for open public accommodations for black students on his college campus.

Unequal treatment in college also goaded others into action. One judge claimed that he "was the first one ever to start a confrontation with the president and hierarchy of a university. I organized a club that went to the president of Harvard University...to open the doors of the dormitories to black students and got 'em open." Another respondent, from a family very active in the struggle for civil rights, did not himself become active until he was in college. "There were problems," he said, "in where a person could get a haircut, where a person could enjoy himself, the whole problem of participation..." He joined with other black students to change the situation. Finally one judge was driven into civil rights ac tivity by the "filthy" restrooms in a segregated moviehouse. "We got them to clean 'em up and make sure that they were clean. And that's where I made my first contact with the NAACP." He later helped to form that organization's first college chapter.

Concern for racial equality is no abstract theory for these black judges. They have not merely been active in civil rights organizations; they have tasted discrimination firsthand. But there have been significant changes in racial behavior in the last quarter-century, and these judges are now leaders of their communities. Nevertheless, recent changes have neither brought full equality to Afro-Americans, nor have they erased race from the consciousness of Afro-American judges. The same racial concern that goaded the respondents into the fight for black equality has surfaced in their socialization and recruitment. Since judges are sworn to uphold the American Constitution which is color-blind, this passion over race may make it difficult for black judges to remain impartial on the bench. Yet their great association with civil rights groups espousing quintessentially American assumptions and ideals may make them succumb presumptively to the traditional role of the judge. In such cases, they are likely to suffer the flak of militant blacks. This conflict between racial sensitivity and professional norms, however, may be clarified by black judges' views of their judicial duties.

Chapter 7
Judicial Attitudes of Black Judges

In the last half of the twentieth century, American society has been forced to undergo a dramatic change in racial etiquette. Partisans for racial justice have petitioned in the courts, lobbied in the legislatures, and marched in the streets, to reshape the political system. Though some of these efforts were successful, significant problems of race remain unsolved. For example, while *de jure* segregation by race has been declared unconstitutional, de facto race separation flourishes in many aspects of American life. We now consider the perspective from which black judges view the races, the courts, and themselves. In particular, these jurists provide a series of related responses on the saliency of racial progress and of the appropriate judicial reaction. This examination is especially relevant because the changes of the last few years may have tinged the self-image of the black bench, whose members have themselves been among the beneficiaries of recent racial advances.

Our attempt to assay the influence of race and robe upon the beliefs of the black bench has thus far been very one-sided. These respondents have repeatedly emphasized the affects of race on their lives and even on their careers. Their insistency has been so strong and so pervasive that we may be forced to exclaim that they are suffering from *race colic*, to paraphrase my grandmother. However, investigating their job attitudes, we find that the constraints of their robes have quietly and stealthily crept into the beliefs of black judges, like a fog on cat's paws. There are indications, moreover, that the mesh of race and robe is a fitful one. The ambivalence of the members of the black bench is most notable in their heightened sense of judicial activism, though they do not follow their own preachings. The sway of their race over the restraints of their robes is, nevertheless, so strong that even now they see themselves as more active than their brethren and appear to strain at the seams for greater bench activity.

As seen in the previous chapter, almost nine out of every ten Afro-American jurists were moderately or very active in the civil rights movement before ascending to the bench. They not only witnessed the racial changes in the society; they helped engineer them. Possibly their great sensitivity to race has not been fully satisfied with the results. Almost 55 percent of the black judges declared that there had been "very much" racial progress in the last twenty years. But, significantly, 44 percent thought there had been only "some" improvement in race relations. This latter group may be a much more demanding lot that still reads of racial differences in income, jobs, housing, and crime statistics. While many of these respondents have achieved rapid advancements in their profession, the latter group of judges may be having doubts about the opportunities available to other blacks, even in the aftermath of the civil rights upheavals of the 1950s and the 1960s. And finally, less than 2 percent asserted that there had been no racial progress in the last two decades.

Even those black jurists who thought the country had achieved great progress in racial affairs must not be mistaken as overly optimistic. When asked to gauge the future racial outlook for the nation, almost 95 percent of the black judges thought America still has a very long journey to travel before achieving racial equality. This finding has significant implications about how these judicial officers perceive the status of American blacks, even today after three decades of progress. It implies that they may be highly sensitive to race in the performance of their judicial duties. In addition, it may be rather surprising that these respondents felt this way, given their own success and power. Some studies have found, along with black folklore, that the more successful blacks become, the less likely they are to identify with their black roots. While this finding does not explicitly refute that notion, it does so implicitly. Of course, there could possibly be extenuating circumstances that distinguish these from other successful blacks. Politically active people are more aware of political currents than the politically inactive. Many of these respondents were active in both civil rights and politics, which possibly heightened their awareness of the gap separating blacks and whites. Five percent of them thought the country had just "some" distance to go before realizing racial equality, though one judge remarked that the United States had reached racial parity. Finally, the responses to this question clash with the answers given by whites, as seen in chapter 1.

As noted earlier, the civil rights movement was for a long time mainly focused on the American judiciary. Indeed, many of the movement's most spectacular victories were won in the courts, with the 1954 Supreme Court decision outlawing segregated schools being the most prominent example. The judiciary has been seen widely as a friend of blacks. One judge aptly illustrated this belief by quoting "the old saying": The American Indian has been a ward of the United States government and the black man has been a ward of the Supreme Court of the United States. Thus, it may come as a surprise to find that less than a quarter of black judges (23 percent) thought that trial courts had made a substantial contribution to the achievement of racial progress.

While a minute 6 percent believed that trial courts had made no contribution, slightly over 70 percent thought they had made some contribution to achieving racial equality. This finding on trial courts is less surprising when it is remembered that many of the far-reaching and widely publicized judicial decisions involving blacks were settled at appellate levels. However, the less prestigious trial courts make numerous less publicized decisions daily. Our respondents who as judges and practicing attorneys, have an intimate knowledge of trial courts, think of them as conservative institutions.

Though lower courts were niggardly in their contribution to racial equality, most were not perceived as highly racist. Only one in seven black judges (less than 15 percent) thought that racism was high in the courts of their communities. Approximately two fifths each saw it as moderate and as low. Given the racial disparities discussed in chapter 1, these may be optimistic assessments of the racial situations in their localities. Yet most interviewees argued that court racism was moderate to low because urban areas, at least in the North, presently have such large black populations "and even more importantly, there are enough black judges on the bench now to keep 'em honest." One easterner who thought judicial racism was moderate pointed, as an example, to the neglect of drug abuse while it was confined to black urban slums. But when drug use spread to "little blonde-haired Sally Ann and little Johnny from the suburbs," rehabilitation programs proliferated.

Race discrimination was not high in their community courts but almost two fifths of all black judges thought there was class discrimination. "We must admit poverty is a big factor (in getting fair treatment). Shouldn't be, it's wrong, but . . . " As examples, some interviewees pointed to the judicial discretion to set bail, to sentence, and to allow warrantless police arrests as examples of discrimination against the poor. "It's the problem generally," conceded one judge on class bias; "he who has the ability to command the best services, will get the best services." While half of the respondents maintained that the poor litigant is treated fairly in their community courts, half also said they found inequitable sentences between the poor and the rich. A Mid-Atlantic judge, in pondering this problem, recalled the case of the soon-to-be 22-year-old defendant who had been convicted but not yet sentenced. Her affluent family avoided the legal question of which of two statutes applied to her by having a private psychologist prepare a sentencing recommendation for the judge. This privately funded report, which was accepted by the presiding judge, saved the defendant from being sentenced under the harsh statute applicable to those 22 years and older.

These two positions of class equality and inequitable sentences seem to be contradictory. Yet they are not alone in their seeming inconsistency. Over half of the black bench (55 percent) asserted that blacks were also treated fairly in the judicial system, though 42 percent affirmed that there were racially inequitable sentencing. An easterner who combined both positions, cited as an example the fact that, in his jurisdiction, the majority of probation oficers are white. They are, he believed, likely to be more interested in a white defendant than a black one. They "would be more apt to put his case in a more favorable light, spend more energy in developing a program of rehabilitation," and in selling it to the judge than if the defendant were black. The white is thus saved from incarceration, while the black goes to prison. In other words, like busy executives everywhere, the harried judge facing an unending docket is at the mercy of his assistants.

It may be that the former assertions on both class and race involved general perceptions, whereas the latter evoked memories of discrete cases. Even so, the willingness of black judges to concede to the presence of class bias in the judiciary is disconcerting, since economic discrimination may be nothing more than race prejudice in a new garb.

While trial court racism was viewed as moderate to low, when the respondents are probed as to how much lower tribunals should offer to race advancement, we spot the first glimmerings that black judges are straining against the traditions of their robes. Over three quarters of them (77 percent) advocated substantial contributions by trial tribunals to race progress, with a fifth more praying for some supplement. Only two of the respondents denied any exertion whatever. The black bench may be gearing up to provide this substantial thrust to race equality.

Most personally interviewed respondents also affirmed that courts should make significant contributions to race achievements, though their reasons were rather varied. Most spoke of the courts' traditional role of protecting the rights of blacks and other minorities. A judge in the East noted the many cases, both national and local, in which the courts had played a leading role. But one of his peers took another view of the traditional role of the judiciary vis-a-vis blacks. He thought that trial courts should make substantial contributions

> because it seems like one of the things that has held racial equality back is fairness in the administration of justice. It is meaningless to say that laws are applied fairly and squarely, and then when you get to an actual judicial system, you get one result in the case of a white defendant and another result in the case of a black defendant.

A jurist from the Mid-Atlantic region declared that courts are an instrument of societal control, and he thought that all such instruments of control and power should be utilized in "our fight for justice and equality."

Another advocate of judicial contributions to racial progress viewed the law "perhaps somewhat egotistically (as) the leading profession for social change." The judge is the pinnacle of the profession. "If he does not lead, who should?"

Only one interviewee thought that trial courts should make only some contribution to the cause of racial equality. he repeatedly emphasized that the judiciary was only one branch of the tripartite system of government. "And where there are racial inequities, any institution that is a forum for the rights of people has a responsibility to provide some leadership. . . " But when pressed as to why "some," this judge invoked judicial restraint. "There's a limitation as to how far trial courts should go and how effective they can be."

While a few of these black judges questioned the effectiveness of the courts, a very substantial number saw judgeships as important instruments for realizing black equality and progress. Indeed, almost all of the respondents (97 percent) took this view, indicating that they saw themselves as powerful actors in the American polity, at least at their local levels. Only five judges denied any such power to their positions.

When queried as to why judgeships are important, the responses were varied. "The whole political superstructure," a young judge asserted, "evolves around the judicial system." The importance of the courts is underlined, in his estimation, by the fact that Congress explicitly reserved its power to appoint judges to the District of Columbia Superior courts, while delegating almost other powers to the local government. Black politicians, he continued, are now aware that "your political power (is) reflected in the judicial branch. . . All the political power in the world can be completely negated in one court order or one court procedure." This judge-centered view is apparently more prevalent among bench members than laymen. For instance, less than half (46 percent) of jurists thought that black politicians were aware of the importance of the judiciary, and less than a quarter (24 percent) felt the average black shared this view. These important actors are, by their own admission, rather isolated in the importance they ascribed to their forums.

Given the power of the courts in fact, it is surprising that most respondents argue in symbols—the mere presence of the black judge enhances the chance for justice for blacks. As one arbiter remarked,

> It means a lot to a black person to walk in a courtroom before a black judge. It gives him a feeling that I think it should give him, a feeling that there's a better chance for getting justice.

A midwestern judge elaborated on this theme, though he, like most others, had many reasons, both symbolic and substantive, for thinking that judgeships are important. He listed his reasons:

> The mere presence of the black judge is going to influence his white associates in their thinking. Secondly, because he is in, shall we say, the councils of the mighty, with policies being fixed that's going to control the police department, the prosecutor's office, and so forth, he can make the input that blacks would like to have with respect to the formulation of that policy. And if he's on his toes, he will do that. Thirdly, of course, he serves as a rallying point. . . he gives a sense of dignity to blacks generally, and

particularly to the youngsters from various schools who come down to visit the courts. . . When they see the black judge there in the flesh, they realize there's hope for them, that they might also one day achieve their highest ambition.

The degree and intensity with which these respondents argued for the presence of blacks on the bench cannot be overemphasized. One District of Columbia judge thought that justice and the judicial system were improved because the black judge brings "an understanding, an awareness, and a sensitivity not only to legal questions and issues but to people who are the main ingredients in a legal system. . ." A Philadelphian asserted that the presence of the black judge "has done more than anything I know to reduce police brutality and to reduce illegal arrests and things of that sort."

This theme of greater and improved justice was cited often, though whether it is true is beyond the scope of this study. Also frequently cited was the theme of black judges as positive models for black youth. This was almost invariably the first response given during the interviews. Though they may sound like retread grist from an old-fashioned integrationist mill, symbols cannot be lightly dismissed in an age of public relations and media "hype." A third theme, that black judges influence policy, was less pronounced, though one judge did mention his court's influence upon the employment practices in the judicial system and collateral institutions as a source of power.

The judiciary is an influential institution in the lives of all Americans. This is particularly true for blacks who constitute a disproportionate number of the litigants appearing before urban courts, especially criminal divisions. And there is ample evidence of racial discrimination in the judicial process, a phenomenon these black judges are acutely aware of. The desire to change the status of Afro-Americans permeates their backgrounds, their judicial recruitment, and their judicial role perceptions. Yet, the role of the judge is probably the most rigorously prescribed one in American society. The exhortations to be fair, impartial, and precedent-oriented, are continually inculcated in law school and in law practice. The black judge may thus be considered a symbol of the conflicting loyalties of race and of professional norm.

The confinement of the robe on the Afro-American jurist can be gleamed even more particularly than seen thus far. And again, the issue is scored by the tension between "is" and "ought." While somewhat more than a quarter (27 percent) observed that black judges do in fact exercise their powers with a special view of protecting the rights of blacks, 40 percent said they themselves did so. However, 45 percent say that black judges ought to wield their authority in such a manner. While 4 percent did not know and 2 percent embraced both poles of "yes and no," 49 percent bellowed negatively. The percentage difference is not great between what they do and what they ought to do, but there seems to be a barrier that restrains them from practicing their own message. Apparently, there is friction between their positions as Afro-Americans and as judges. Yet it is remarkable that so few respondents feel responsible for protecting black rights, considering the effects even today of the intense, systematic, and long-term exclusion of blacks from American society. However, it may be equally remarkable that so few responded negatively, given the highly touted judicial traits of restraint, impartiality, and reliance on precedents.

Some of the interviewees answering affirmatively believed in enhancing the rights of all criminal defendants. As a consequence, they were protecting the rights of blacks. A Michigander stated that black judges ought to declare that "everybody's going to get equal justice," by saying that, "you're going to give blacks something that they haven't been getting in the past." But one District of Columbia liberal took a special view "because the rights of blacks have historically (been) overlooked and disregarded."

Respondents who answered negatively disliked the idea of racial favoritism. "Be fair and be impartial," enjoined a Baltimorean. A neighboring Democrat argued that "there is (only) so much that can be done within the framework and interpretation of the Constitution." And many considered themselves to be judges for all people, not for black exclusively: "I don't consider myself a black judge; I consider myself a judge."

Among both the advocates and opponents of a protective treatment of black litigants, many qualified their responses. The former believed their duty "must be affirmative." Offended by some of his brethren's highly publicized racial postures, a Mid-Atlantic Democrat qualified his affirmative answer because

> you can utilize your position to be an effective force for the black community and black defendant without being an asinine, arbitrary, biased bastard in reverse. . . A guy's got to be very technical and subtle about how he handles it.

He asserted that judges must consider the handicaps under which blacks labor.

Judges on both sides of this issue spoke sensitively about the plight of Afro-Americans. When queried as to why he responded negatively, one interviewee exlaimed, "Because I answered the question in the briefest possible way so I could get rid of that damn thing and get it back to you." His annoyance aside, the disposition of each judge influenced his reply. The factors that shaped such dispositions call for further investigation, which we will attempt to pinpoint in subsequent chapters.

Since these judges favor bench activity that admittedly they do not practice to the fullest extent, it should come as no surprise to find that they shift their ideological gears once they are on the court. As shown earlier, they tended to describe themselves overwhelmingly as political liberals (63 percent) and moderates (30 percent), with a minuscule number of conservatives and others (8 percent). Even so, the influence of the bench has moderated their outlook, though age and other factors may have also intervened. Though a majority (53 percent) consider themselves liberals in their judicial ideology, some members of the group have muted their progressive-activist faith. Two fifths said that they were judicial moderates, with 7 percent opting for a variety of hyphenated hybrids. As in other areas of judicial attitude, the percentage differences are not egregious. Nevertheless, they are indications of the degree to which the seemingly race-motivated activism of black judges is being enthralled by their robe.

The traditional role of the judge has dampened the fires of Afro-American arbiters, but it has not completely extinguished them. Even though they are ambivalent about espousing a special protective role of black litigants, do not always practice what they advocate, and have softened their ideology once on the judiciary, the sensitivity to race exhibited throughout their lives and careers is still transformed into an applause for judicial activism far outstripping anything found for comparable white judges.

When queried about general judicial role perceptions, for instance, over a third (36 percent) voted for judicial innovation. While less than a fifth (18 percent) believed that judges should merely apply the law, another third took a position "in-between" these two poles. One judge thought that "each has its place." Another "in-between" based his judicial activity upon "a gut reaction to what you think is right." The weakness or strength of precedents are the guideposts for a liberal Democratic judge. Innovation is a peculiar advantage of the American judiciary, said one moderate Republican, "because the law can expand or contract" as the times require. Another GOP moderate favored innovation because "the law is evolving." This latter Republican advocated innovation from the bench because "black folks have not been treated fairly in the status quo." Another inteviewee spoke of the "obligation" to initiate "a change in the law which will be beneficial to the groups that have been the victims of injustice in the past."

Obviously, race is a factor in the judicial activism of these black judges, most of whom sit on trial benches. A similar study by Ish of mostly white trial judges did not find such an extensive belief in court activism. For instance, while only 18 percent of black judges favored the judicial restraint position of applying the law, Ish found that almost two thirds of judges in San Francisco and Baltimore metropolitan areas advocated a comparable position. Over a third of the Afro-American bench believed in the activist position of innovation; only a twentieth of the Ish sample supported a comparable stance. Quite likely, these great differences are explained by the difference in race. Of Ish's fifty-nine respondents, three were black, and in an uncanny coincidence only three of his judges chose judicial activism.

When asking the percentage of cases that offer any real opportunity for innovation, we get an idea of the pedestrian nature of judging in American courts, at least at the lower levels. Two thirds of the ebon bench specified "a few," "some," and up to 10 percent. Thirty percent noted from a tenth to infrequent citations of three quarters and "most," with only 3 percent saying that "none" does.

The friction between the race and the robe of Afro-American jurists surfaces again when questioned about judicial policymaking. They provide further evidence that these arbiters are more zealous in this controversial area than their white brethren, but are not as aggressive as they would like to be. For instance, only 7 percent of the respondents believed that judges on their court level substantially attempt to make public policy, with an additional three fifths discerning some effort to do so. The remaining number, almost a third, declared that their fellow adjudicators made no such attempt. However, when asked what they themselves do, 16 percent checked substantially attempt and almost two thirds make some exertion to shape public programs. Thus, these judges see themselves as more aggressive than their fellow jurists. But the final wrinke is that a full quarter of them affirmed that they and their bench-mates should make great efforts to mold the political and social policies which come before them. Over three fifths avowed that they ought to make some initiative in such areas, and only 14 percent renounced any exercise whatsoever.

No previous study of the judiciary has found judges having such a belief in the active power of the trial bench, or even the appellate one. When asked for examples of their judicial policymaking, many of the respondents who were personally interviewed cited their handling of police brutality and illegal arrest cases. Their treatment of such cases informs the respective police departments and prosecutor's offices of judicially acceptable behavior. one judge went so far as to announce from his bench that all parties injured in resisting arrest cases would be freed. His rationale was that the police had already inflicted punishment. One Marylander recalled his ruling that prisoners have the right to receive their mail uncensored and to have articulate, though nonlawyer, counsel present at prison grievance hearings. Probably the most far-reaching example of judicial policymaking was offered by a Philadelphia judge who wrote the decision mandating legal assistance for the poor. His decision was later affirmed by the United States Supreme Court.

Given the liberal uses that the activist-oriented black judges would like to carry to the courts, it probably comes as little surprise to find that a majority of them (54 percent) considered the judiciary to be a political institution. "They are controlled as a result of political power," rationalized one interviewee from the District of Columbia. While 14 percent did not respond to this query, the remaining 32 percent denied that courts were political, at least not in partisan party terms. For instance, one such demurrer wrote confidentially that "I hear they are in Illinois and New York."

The enormous race sensitivity of the black bench is testament to what white Americans have made of race. Though a third of all the respondents denied experiencing any discrimination on the bench, from a fifth to a tenth swore that they had suffered such bias from white politicians, from the press, from police, from bar members, and from fellow judges. Though he was quick to laud the chief administrative judge for the impartial assignment of cases, a moderate Republican who claimed discrimination from other sources commented, "It's not the type of thing you could point a hard finger at. Black folks are generally discriminated against, and it's no different for judges." Thus, paranoia may have to be added to the schizoid conflict of race and robe, even though, to paraphrase the recent joke, just because you are paranoid does not mean they are not discriminating against you.

Race is a constant factor in the lives of black jurists. It would, however, be a mistake to confuse the race consciousness of these respondents with race bias in the performance of their official duties. Though a mere 6 percent declared themselves to be "black judges," more than 9 out of 10 maintained that they are "judges who are black." In the recent past, the enduring schism in the black community between nationalists and integrationists found an outlet in this type of labeling. The overwhelming majority of the black bench remained true to their integrationist faith, and to their NAACP membership card, in emphasizing that they were judges who were black. In any case, the quest for racial justice characterized both groups.

Indeed, the notion of justice for "blacks and all others" is a consistent thread throughout the lives, careers, and attitudes of the black judiciary. When asked, for example, for the impact of a black judge on the black community, almost two fifths (37 percent) sounded variations on the theme of justice. A quarter insisted that their presence insures a "fair deal," with an additional 12 percent noting that the black judge "gives protection." A third justified their position on the bench by claiming that they provide symbolic pride, inspiration, and status for American blacks. Only 9 percent denied any such significance at all, while the remaining number did not discern any distinctions.

Declarations of justice again crop up when the ebon jurists are questioned about their contributions to the general community. A third testified that their appearance on the courts improved equity, with an additional 14 percent saying that the bench was more representative of the general community. Of the remainder, a fifth noted some, little, or no distinctness; an additional fifth chose "other," a variegated category; and 12 percent did not know of any contribution to the community in general.

Meting out justice is the most important responsibility of the black judge—71 percent said as much. In addition, others declared that the arbiter must "balance needs," "protect litigants," "weigh all factors," and "conform with and encourage respect for the law." Two fifths disclosed that sentencing is the hardest part of their job, though achieving fairness is the difficult part for 5 percent. Others have trouble "reaching decisions" or "remaining objective" or "determining facts" or coping with court congestion. Finally, a fifth of the black bench pronounced that the best part of their judgeship is meting out justice, with a quarter more pointing to the rehabilitation of convicts or serving the community. Some enjoy trial work, while for others, the power or salary or prestige of a judgeship is important.

As we glance at the significance of judicial duties to black judges, we find that they are not radically different from their fellows in some respects. They recite the same gripes and project the same joys as white judges. Above all, they seek justice, for blacks as well as whites. They only differ from white judges in their advocacy of bench activism.

The concern for racial equality in the courts leads the Afro-American jurists to strain the seams of their robes. They envision the judiciary as an arena for the achievement of racial progress; they thus urge judicial energy to meet this goal. Race is their concern; the court is their rampart. The judicial role, which had been noticeably absent in their lives and careers, restrains their judicial enthusiasm. The traditional role of the judge seems too narrow for their concern, energy, and activity.

Yet race and role vary from one individual to another. In an effort to assay the weight of these and other factors, we now correlate selected variables with the self-images of black judges.

Chapter 8
Socioeconomic Factors and Judicial Attitudes

Afro-Americans have long been mesmerized by models since this is the age of symbolism. The "first" black to play major league baseball and the "first" black to be awarded the Nobel Peace Prize are examples. Indeed, even black judges tend to justify their positions symbolically. But the saliency of signs is not confined to blacks exclusively; modern social science has also come under its sway. Socioeconomic attributes are one of the inevitable features of social analysis. Even though they mask a variety of life-styles and personalities, they are investigated because they are assumed to be symbolic or indicative of outlooks and behavior. Factors such as social origin, age, sex, and diverse affiliations, are indications of how social systems operate. An examination of elite backgrounds can thus illuminate the impact of societal values on the attitudes of black judges.

FAMILY STATUS

The family is quite possibly the foremost influence on the life of the child. Parents are important because they (1) represent a system of social, moral, and personal values, and (2) utilize specific techniques or practices of child-rearing that often have permanent effects on the young. Families influence their children's personalities, career choices, political values, and political party identifications. Given all this, one would expect to find a positive relationship between the social backgrounds and role perceptions of black judges. In fact, this is not the case. Relationships between the two variables were neither as consistent nor as pronounced as expected.

Moving to the first correlation, the self-described social backgrounds of blacks is significantly related to their views of racial progress. Having dropped the category of "none" because of low cell frequencies, the measure of significance is .03, which is below the acceptable maximum of .05 discussed in chapter 2. In addition, the strength of the relationship of class to views of racial progress is slightly less than .10 (Kendall's Tau c = .09), whereas the intensity of an association is noted by its closeness to 1.0. Even so, those black judges from working-class backgrounds were evenly divided concerning the amount of racial progress that has been achieved in the last twenty years. But 60 percent of those from nonworking middle/upper-class families felt there had been a great deal of racial progress. Though it could be assumed that those from the lower class, having come a greater social distance, would check "very much," they did so significantly less than their higher-class brethren. There are possible explanations for this apparent anomaly. First, having come a greater social distance, the working-class judge is likely to have family members and friends whose life-styles have not substantially improved in recent years. A second possible explanation is similar to the first: the middle/upper-class respondents were more likely to know people from comparable backgrounds and to have seen them improve their socioeconomic positions as well. A third explanation may be that black jurists from middle/upper-class families were in a better position than their less-fortunate neighbors to realize the fruits of the civil rights movement. It could be argued that they were more prepared for advancement than lower-class respondents since they had hurdled all barriers, except the racial one. Having overcome that obstacle, they were inclined to be optimistic in assessing recent racial progress.

When asked how pervasive racism is in the courts of their community, the working-class black judges gave lower estimates of racism than did their middle/upper-class counterparts, however. Approximately the same percentage of respondents (15 percent) from both classes thought racial discrimination in the local courts was high. Though half of the middle/upper-class offsprings saw it as moderate, a considerable number (44 percent) of the products of working-class families agreed. The five or so percentage points separating the two class groups in asserting that court racism is moderate to low, accounts for the lack of significance (p = .22) and of strength (Kendall's Tau c = .04) in this association. This finding does not comport with the class alignment found on racial progress. While the two are not synonymous, they are closely related. Moreover, there are no ready explanations for this seeming discrepancy.

All class lines disappeared, however, when black judges were asked whether they should extend special protection to the rights of black litigants. As seen earlier, the black bench is split down the middle on this controversial query. In correlating class with a special view, the test of association is infinitesimal (Cramer's V = .002) and significance is astronomical (p = .49). The question is so loaded, with so many professional and societal implications, that the social backgrounds of the respondents provide no cue to their responses. Both working-class and middle/upper-class judges are so evenly distributed, pro and con, on this issue, that only one percentage point separates them. For instance, 49 percent of working-class judges and 48 percent of middle/upper-class judges pledged that the black bench should exercise its powers with a special view of protecting the rights of blacks, with the remaining numbers dissenting.

It is possible that professional socialization has a much greater relationship to this special protection query than does family status and its more general socialization. The responses may be more influenced by adult rather than childhood learning. Finally, the issue itself is too ambiguous, especially since many of the respondents penned "yes and no" in the margins of the questionnaire.

While class lines were submerged and indistinct on the black protection question, status distinctions are the clearest thus far on the question of attitudes toward judicial innovation. The test of significance yields a highly acceptable four out of one thousand probability of sampling error, and the relationship though low, is the strongest of any yet found (Tau c = −.15). Black judges from working-class backgrounds are much more likely to advocate judicial activism than those from nonworking-class families. Conversely, the working-class respondents were less likely to opt for applying the law or taking the in-between position than their bourgeois counterparts. Over a quarter of the middle/upper-class judges believed that judges were limited to applying the law as compared to less than 18 percent of the working-class judges. Slightly more than a third of the children of working-class backgrounds chose the in-between position, but just over two fifths of their bourgeois counterparts did.

Given the previous ambiguity in class correlations, this clear-cut, significant relationship between attitudes toward judicial activism and class is rather surprising and not easily explained. It may be said that the black middle-class is more conservative and more "rule" oriented than the working-class members. Since the association of class and racial progress was also found to be significant, this latest discovery may be just an indication of the alienation of working-class black judges. The other side of the coin is that the middle class could be more satisfied with the political and legal situation in the country than their less-advantaged brothers. This angle, however, flies in the face of numerous instances of bourgeois leaders and members who attack social problems.

Since the relationship between social class and attitudes toward judicial activism was significant, it is somewhat surprising to find no relationship between class and the related question of willingness to make public policy. The test for statistical significance yields a high, and highly unacceptable, .40. The relationships are much more mixed than was the case of attitudes toward judicial legislation. Even given the lack of significance and strength, the working-class jurists were more inclined to favor judicial activism than those from the middle class. Just over a quarter (27 percent) gave their nod to substantial attempts to formulate policies from the bench, while less than a fifth (22 percent) of the middle-class respondents agreed. However, lower-class arbiters were also more disposed to make no attempt at initiating bench policy (16 percent) compared to those of the middle class (12 percent). Two thirds of middle/upper-class judges were favorably tilted to courts composing some public policy, and 57 percent of the children of laborers were. There is thus no consistent association of social class and perceptions of judicial policymaking.

Nevertheless, scanning all the correlations, a pattern emerges of the middle-class jurists; they believed that court racism was moderate, that judges should straddle the chasm between innovating and applying the law, and that judges should make "some" attempts to devise public policy.

In this series of correlations, the findings generally have been mixed; though there are indications that family status has some influence on the role attitudes of black judges. The most notable results appear to be that jurists from the black working class are more likely than their middle/upper-class peers to feel that judges should be activists on the bench. Even so, a significant relationship was found on only one of the activism dimensions, though that was a highly significant and moderately strong one.

Although some observers have seen the family as the major influence on the political life of the child, others, such as Jennings and Niemi, have minimized this relationship, arguing that, except for party affiliation, the family "transmits its own particular values in relatively few areas of political socialization." Given the questionable habit of inferring political values from socio-economic back-grounds and the decidedly mixed correlations found in this examination, their qualms may be justified. Socialization is a continuous process, and the family is only one of several socializing agents. Religion is another, and we now turn to investigate its influence on the role perceptions of the members of the black judiciary.

RELIGIOUS AFFILIATIONS

Religious affiliation may indicate a person's attitudes, beliefs, and practices toward God, but it often indicates something more—social status. Lazerwitz found that education, occupation, and income, sorted religious groups into a social hierarchy, with Episcopalians, Presbyterians, and Jews at the top; Methodists, Lutherans, and Roman Catholics in the middle; and Baptists at the bottom. Other students of the social basis of religion, Gockel being one of the most recent, have reached the same general conclusions. Moreover, studies of elite decision-makers have found that the high-status denominations are overrepresented at the highest levels of the public and private sectors. Even given the Protestant Ethic, it would appear unlikely that religious affiliation would explain such achievements. Gockel finds that the differences in income among religious groups are related to occupation and education, and not to religious affiliation. Quite possibly, the high-status religious denominations enhance their standing through the recruitment of the upwardly mobile. Warren provides evidence that such people change their religion to reflect their new, more prestigious status.

As seen in chapter 3, many of these black judges have generally changed their religious affiliation from Baptist to Methodist to Presbyterian and Episcopalian. While the reasons for this conversion were diverse, the net result was that many of these judges now hold church membership commensurate with their professional and social status.

Using Gockel's finding that income is related to occupation and education, and not to religion, we would assume that religious affiliation does not influence the role perceptions of black judges. This assumption could be justified on two other grounds. For one, the influence of religious affiliation upon judicial attitudes may be minimized since it is, for Sheldon Goldman, "much too broad a variable encompassing a multitude of individual experiences and (is) thus affected by a host of intervening variables." This injunction may apply even more since race would be one of these intervening variables. For another, Hacker has noted that the traditional social hierarchy of religions may not apply to white southerners because of the predominance of the Baptist denomination in the region. For the same reason, it may not apply to black Americans.

On the other hand, some studies of nonblack judges have found relationships between religious affiliation and judicial behavior. For instance, Sheldon Goldman, assuming that religion was too diffuse in its impact to affect judicial voting behavior, still discovered that federal appellate judges of the Catholic and Jewish faiths voted more liberally for the economic underdog. These studies treated Catholics and Jews as minority faiths and "possibly more socialized to favor the underdog."

Our own study concerns the attitudes of black appellate and trial judges. Given the conclusions of previous studies, religion as an influence upon the role perceptions of black judges is ripe for examination.

Warren has complained of the enduring Catholic-Protestant dichotomy and blamed it on the collapsing of Protestants into one group because of the low cell frequencies of some Protestant denominations. Our examination does not collapse Protestants and suffers from a low cell frequency. Thus we will not be able to give statistical significance or the strength of the relationship observed in some instances. Though our findings will not be conclusive, they may spur others to more detailed research of the influence of religion on judges and other decision-makers.

Examining the correlations, there are no substantial indications that religious affiliations mold the role perceptions of black judges. However, the Catholic respondents appear to favor judicial restraint and, more interestingly, those with no declared religious affiliations seem inclined to believe in judicial activism.

Catholics, Methodists, and "others," tend to think that an appreciable degree of racial progress has been achieved in the last twenty years. Presbyterians were the least likely to have seen substantial advancements in race relations (44 percent), compared to 65 percent for Catholics and 60 percent for both "others" and Methodists. The most popular denomination among black jurists, the Baptist, was split evenly, with nonaffiliated registering 53 percent and Episcopalians at 48 percent. Even though those replying that they have observed some and no race progress, have been collapsed into one category, the test of association yields no significance (p = .80) and a strength of .13.

When asked their view of the level of racism in their community court system, almost a third (31 percent) of the judges professing no religious affiliations asserted it to be high. They were followed in this assessment by Episcopalians (23 percent) and by Catholics (17 percent). Approximately a tenth of Methodist (12 percent) and Presbyterians (11 percent) concurred. Yet 8 percent of the Baptists and 6 percent of "others" saw judicial racism as high.

Moving to the backside of the correlation, a quarter of the nonaffiliated discerned court bias as low. They were the least likely to state this position among the denominations surveyed. For example, the religious groups closest to this view were the Presbyterians with a third and "others" with two fifths nodding agreement. All other denominations were somewhat more optimistic in this low assessment—ranging from Episcopalians at 42 percent to Baptists at 45 percent.

The array of religionists who viewed court discrimination as moderate is bewildering. Almost three fifths (56 percent) of both Presbyterians and "others" checked this middle option; while at the other end, a third of the Episcopalians assented. The inchoate pattern of Presbyterian race consciousness sighted on the race progress question has proved on court racism to be an ephemeral one. Chi-square, the test of significance, is not reported for this correlation because the distribution of the marginal frequencies did not provide sufficiently large expected cell frequencies. We have run into the problem that Warren forewarned when treating religious denominations separately in a relatively small survey.

Focusing on questions of judicial duties, a pattern emerges in which restraint is embraced by black Catholic judges and activity by nonaffiliated ones. When asked, for instance, whether they should be especially conscientious toward protecting the rights of blacks who come before their benches, almost two thirds (65 percent) of the Catholic adherents answered negatively. Yet they were counterbalanced by nearly two thirds (65 percent) of the judges with no church membership. While Baptists jurists tended to think they should take an extraordinary stance (58 percent), their brethren in the Presbyterian, Episcopalian, and Methodist faiths were opposed (61 percent, 58 percent, and 58 percent, respectively). Those in "other" denominations were almost evenly divided (53 percent for and 47 percent against) on this troublesome issue of a special protective role for black judges of black litigants. While this array, or rather disarray, is puzzling, it is not statistically significant (p = .38).

When asked if they believe in applying the law, innovating, or a position in-between, black Catholic judges again tended to favor restraint from the judiciary, while the nonreligionists clung to the opposite pole. A third of the former thought they should apply the law, which is widely considered to be a conservative position; and only a fifth opted for judicial innovation, a "liberal" posture. On the other hand, less than a fifth (19 percent) of those professing no church allegiance would apply the law, but over two thirds (69 percent) believed in charting new legal paths. Those respondents in "other" denominations were least likely of all to state that judges should follow the law as given—not one checked this option. Although 8 percent of the Baptists embraced such judicial restraint, almost a quarter of both the Episcopalians and the Methodists preferred this approach to adjudicating. Presbyterians were sharply divided. While 39 percent adopted the conservative pose, 54 percent selected innovation from the bench. They were the staunchest defenders of judicial restraint and the second greatest advocates of judicial invention. Baptists, with 45 percent, were next in line in asserting legal pathbreaking, followed by approximately two fifths of "others" (41 percent) and Methodist (38 percent). The religionists who nodded to the moderate stance of in-between were led by "others" (59 percent). Baptist, Catholics, Episcopalians, and Methodists, ranged from almost half to a third straddling the middle-of-the-road. Presbyterians (8 percent) and nonaffiliates (13 percent) were least likely to avoid the poles on the question of innovation.

Out of this welter of numbers, nonaffiliates and Presbyterians emerged as most inclined to choose judicial change. This pattern continues when the judges are interrogated as to what extent they should attempt to formulate public policy. Somewhat less than a third (29 percent) of the followers of John Calvin opined that judges should substantially seek to shape public programs; more telling, not one favored no endeavor whatsoever (7 out of 10 affirming moderate bench efforts). Over a quarter (27 percent) of the nonaffiliates agreed with great exertions, along with an equal percentage of Methodists. Catholics and Episcopalians who had previously evinced a distaste for judicial invention, continued in that path. Of all religious groups, these two were least likely to concur with substantial moves to mold policy from the bench (approximately 20 percent for each). Conversely, they were most likely to commend no attempt at all—27 percent of Episcopalians and 20 percent of Catholics. A quarter of Baptists and "others" approved of efforts to devise programs from the bench, though 15 percent of the former and only 5 percent of the latter discouraged such exercises. From somewhat over half to two thirds of Episcopalians, Methodists, Baptists, Catholics, nonaffiliates, and "others," encouraged moderate uses of judicial powers.

In the last two correlations, a test of significance was useless since many expected cell frequencies did not contain the necessary distribution of responses. However, in "eyeballing" the relationships, consistent patterns of the association of religious affiliates with judicial attitudes surfaced. But, they certainly did not prove or even indicate that "high-status" Protestants were conservative. Presbyterians, for example, were most likely to advocate activism from the bench, though Episcopalians were least inclined to aid such efforts. Nor did the sightings indicate that "low-status" Baptists had any enthusiasm for judicial pathbreaking. This is not surprising since Sheldon Goldman found no difference in the voting behavior of high- and low-status Protestant appellate judges. While there were indications of attitudinal differences between black judges of different denominations, they did not emerge along a high- and low-status Protestant continuum.

The nonaffiliates, having already demonstrated a willingness to break the ties that bind in religious matters, favored such freeing of the restraints that tether judges. This advocacy may be linked to an indifference to forms and traditions. "Minority faith" Catholic black judges, whose rituals and tenets emphasize the traditions of their ancient church, somewhat reflected a traditional view of their bench duties in stressing restraint. But, even here, most preferred moderate judicial activity.

The search for affinities between the religious denominations and role perceptions of black judges is hampered by the lack of a test of significance. Thus, despite the conventional wisdom that religion strongly affects the roles and behavior of other black elites in public life, we must conclude that religious affiliation is too broad a variable encompassing too many individual experiences to provide any discernible influence on the bench attitudes of black judges.

AGE

"Never trust anybody over thirty." This phrase was thought by many to characterize the youth movement of the 1960s and early 1970s. Probably uttered half in jest, the injunction has been overworked by American journalists. Youth is seen as a period of liberalism, while maturity is depicted as a period of comparative conservatism. Whether the world can be so neatly categorized is questionable. Glenn has challenged the different definitions of conservatism and the different dimensions of aging. On the other hand, survey research polls have consistently found generational discrepancies on political and social issues. For instance, both blacks and whites under the age of 30 were more likely to believe that marijuana use should be legalized. Those advocating that position become progressively fewer with maturity—47 percent of respondents below 30 and 15 percent of those above 50 favored legalization of marijuana use. A more apt illustration of the relative liberalism of the young is a comparison of blacks and whites on questions of race relations. In early 1981, younger respondents were more inclined than their seniors to disagree with the statement that blacks have less inborn ability to learn than whites or that blacks do not have the willpower to pull themselves out of poverty. After examining political beliefs over a span of twenty years in *The Changing American Voter,* Nie and others had "no doubt that the tendency of the young is to be more liberal than their elders."

Apart from public opinion polls, there have not been many similar findings in studies of the American judiciary. In his earlier examination of the voting behavior of federal appeals courts, Sheldon Goldman found a statistically significant correlation between age and liberal-conservative voting. Since he had found no other solid evidence in judicial behavior literature to support an association between these two variables, he hypothesized in his later federal appellate court studies that no such relationship would be found. But he again found a relationship. Older federal appeals judges tended to be more conservative than their younger fellows on criminal procedure, civil liberties, labor, injured persons, political liberalism, economic liberalism, and activism dimensions. Indeed, age was found to have been the single most important background variable for civil liberties and activism. While Sheldon Goldman studied judicial behavior and this examination of black judges confines itself to attitudes, we believe that age and attitude are related.

Indeed, the relationship between the age and attitudes of black judges is actually among the strongest and most consistent yet uncovered. Younger black judges are inclined to believe in judicial activism; older black judges tend to favor judicial restraint. For example, when asked how much racial progress had occurred in the past twenty years, only half of the jurists thirty-nine years or younger said very much. But almost 70 percent of those sixty years or older thought that substantial racial advancement had developed. This relationship is highly significant (p = .0001) and one of the strongest yet found (Kendall's Tau c = .20). It may be that the older judges are grateful for any improvements in the black condition since they remember when things were much worse; when blacks were restricted in public eating facilities, in travel accommodations, in voting rights, and in job opportunities. These older black judges now see blacks taking seats in Congress, state legislatures, city halls, and even in courthouses. Becoming a judge for most of them must have been a distant, almost unthinkable goal. Now that they sit on the bench, they may place great value in the distances they have traveled. On the other hand, the more junior judges may heed the more militant cry that blacks are not yet full and equal partners in American society. Possibly, they recall that blacks are still disproportionately represented in poverty statistics, in school dropout rates, in criminal arrest records, and in prison populations. The country has made some racial progress, as almost all agree; but the harder, more substantive ground is yet to be traveled. They see things, not as they have been, but as they must become.

However, the highly significant relationship between age and views of racial progress is even more remarkable considering the convoluted patterns found for judges 40-60. Respondents in the age group 40-49 were less likely than their younger colleagues to say that very much race advancement characterized the past twenty years—less than 40 percent affirmed while 61 percent noted some or none. Those judges in the next older age category, 50-59, remained true to the line of progression—the older the judge, the more likely he will find recent race progress. For instance, almost three fifths (58 percent) said there had been substantial race achievement versus over two fifths (42 percent) making a less generous assessment.

When asked if racism was high, moderate, or low in the courts of their community, the relationship of age and racial worlds view is repeated. Almost 70 percent of the eldest jurists thought that court racism was low. Yet, slightly less than 30 percent of the youngest respondents thought likewise. On the other end, less than 4 percent of the most senior arbiters said that judicial race bias was high, while three times as many (12 percent) of the most junior judges felt the same. It is also noteworthy that those in their 40s and 50s were even more likely than the youngest group, those in their 30s, to think that court racism was high. In fact, almost a quarter (24 percent) of the 40-49-year-old black judges said as much. Even those in their 50s were slightly more inclined to discern court discrimination than their youngest brethren—16 percent compared to 12 percent. In addition, a third each of the 40- and 50-year-old jurists detected judicial discrimination as low in their jurisdictions. This association is also very significant (p = .0005) and mildly strong (Kendall's Tau c = .18).

The difference between those judges below 60 years of age and those above is quite distinct in this latter correlation. Sheldon Goldman found the voting differences of his federal appeals judges most noticeable at this demarcation line. Whether a traumatic psychological aging process occurs at this age, even whether a distinct aging process exists, is still uncertain. It may be that people around this age decide to foreswear learning what is currently fashionable. Possibly, at this age they most strongly decide, whether consciously or unconsciously, that the old attitudes and the old ways of living are the best.

For these black judges, the demarcation age of sixty may mask a generational change of consciousness. These seemingly more conservative black jurists are more likely to think that court racism is low because it is no longer as blatant as they remember it. Some of the oldest ones can recall when judges and prosecuting attorneys spoke to them and their clients without using their titles or by using the epithet of *nigger*. They feel that court racism has been lowered by the disappearance of such rude racial behavior, especially since blacks are now treated with more respect and deference at the bar. Having seen those insults overcome, the younger judges have moved on to other racial problems. They are puzzled over the racial disparities in conviction rates and in prison sentences since the courts, an integral part of the criminal process, play a role in these racial disparities. Consequently, the youngest respondents saw court racism as moderate to high because their perspectives were different.

The generational configurations continue on the next correlation, but they are not as significant (p = an acceptable .03) or as strong (Cramer's V = .11) as the previous ones. When asked if they take a special view toward protecting the rights of blacks, slightly less than 30 percent of the judges aged 60 and older answered affirmatively. Yet almost 60 percent of the youngest groups did so.

Conversely, less than 44 percent of the jurists in their 30s and below responded negatively to this "special view" of blacks, while over 70 percent of the eldest group indicated a similar stance. As found in the previous question, the 50-59-age category registered almost as sharp a break with those above their age as do those in the youngest stratum. For instance, 56 percent of them are disposed to exercising their powers with an extraordinary perspective of protecting Afro-American litigants. The seeming militance of those in their 40s, on the other hand, became less pronounced—48 percent of them take a special view versus 52 percent who are opposed. Their sharp split on this query no doubt accounts for the lesser strength and significance of this association than on the previous two. Even so, there is significance uncovered.

When black judges are asked their ideas about judicial activism, the age relationships again become highly significant (p = .0008), though of relatively mild strength (Kendall's Tau c = -.18). Almost 60 percent of those aged 39 and younger favored innovation from the bench, but less than 20 percent of the eldest judges opted for this posture. On the judicial restraint side of the controversy, none of the youngest group believed in merely applying the law, though over 40 percent of the most senior respondents did. As before, the shift in attitude between those above and below age 60 is abrupt and egregious. For instance, over half of the black judges aged 50-59 chose bench pathbreaking, which contrasts markedly with the fifth of those above age 60 who checked this position. And only 17 percent of those in their 50s nodded for the "conservative" stance of applying the law. Moreover, the aggressiveness of respondents in their 40s becomes a memory. They were second to the eldest group in their dislike for charting new legal ground from the bench. Though two fifths would do so, they were far outdistanced by those in their 30s and 50s. Almost half of the 40s (47 percent) division straddled the fence on this issue of judicial decision-making.

Black judges in their 60s and above have given every indication of favoring restraint from the judiciary. Yet they provide some surprises on the last correlation. These surprises are softened somewhat by a fractionally unacceptable statistical significance (p = .08) and by the weakest relationship found in this discussion of age and judicial role attitudes (Kendall's Tau c = -.09). Almost 30 percent of the eldest cluster of black judges admitted that they substantially attempt to chart public policy, while only 13 percent of the youngest set acknowledged the same effort. In fact, there is an ascending order of age and of "substantial" willingness to shape policy from the court—the older the judge, the more likely he is to advocate substantial efforts to formulate public policy. The line progresses from 13 percent for those in their 30s, to 19 percent for the 40s, to 28 percent for the 50s and finally 29 percent for the 60s and above.

Notwithstanding this distinction, the age patterns previously uncovered are still evident in this last correlation, though they are weaker. For example, less than 7 percent of the youngest group of black judges believed in making no attempts at judicial policymaking, but almost 21 percent of their eldest brethren took such a position. Four fifths of the former group said that they attempted "somewhat" to make public policy, and only half of the latter indicated as much.

In this last correlation, the demarcation line of age 60, which generally separated the adherents of judicial activism from those of restraint, is somewhat less evident. Yet the group just below that age (50-59) still tends to favor judicial activism more than those above that age. Almost 30 percent indicated that they substantially attempt to make public policy from the bench and less than 7 percent indicated no such attempt. The 40-49-year-olds show themselves, on all correlations, to be less in favor of judicial activism than the 50-59-age group. For instance, though less than a fifth of the former group (19 percent) chose to substantially attempt policymaking, they were more than balanced by the quarter (24 percent) who said they made no such attempts. The differences in judicial perspectives of the two middle-aged categories are puzzling, and there are no handly explanations for the dissimilarities.

Even more curious is the reversal of the eldest group on the final correlations. One would assume that views of judicial policymaking and views of judicial activism are different aspects of the same question. Yet 30 percent of those age 60 and older believed in substantially attempting to shape policy from the bench, while less than 20 percent favored innovation as a judicial activity. Possibly, there are nuances in the questions or in the experiences of these respondents that underlie this seeming anomaly. Almost all of the eldest judges were in law school or were practicing attorneys at the time of the New Deal. Many may have learned their lessons of judicial restraint from the unpopular, activist Supreme Court of that era.

Notwithstanding these puzzles, our general finding still stands. Age is related to the role perceptions of black judges, unlike either family or religious affiliations. The younger jurists are more likley to favor judicial activism; the eldest ones are more likely to believe in judicial restraint. Furthermore, the age of 60 seems to be the line separating believers in activism from counselors of restraint.

Age as an influence in the judicial process has received increased attention recently. Since it may be one of the most important factors influencing judges and other decision-makers, more research on it is needed.

Chapter 9
Legal Factors and Judicial Attitudes

It is almost a wives' tale that the law is a conservative discipline. There are no major findings to prove this belief, yet it still has wide currency. The legal discipline, with its reliance on prior cases and decisions, often seems to inculcate a preference for what is settled. The law must be stable if it is to be known and obeyed, or so some scholars argue. In an effort to ascertain the weight of various factors on the role perceptions of black judges, their estimation of law school influence, of law school rank, and of law practice, will now be investigated.

LAW SCHOOL INFLUENCE AND RANK

The picture of the law as conservative, and of law schools as the initial professional socializing agents, may be misleading. Lortie, for instance, has found that professional socialization probably occurs more in law practice than in law school. Moreover, there are substantial numbers of liberals found in this study of black judges. In chapter 4, we showed the liberalizing impact of law schools on the civil rights activity and attitudes of black members of the judiciary. It must be assumed that legal education and discipline are not as uniformly influential as many believe, especially since liberal jurists are buttressed in their faith by a long and glorious tradition of dissent in the appellate courts of this country. Dissents are an example of how unsettled the law can be. The law is full of ferment and, if the United States Supreme Court is any indication, generally changes with the times.

The correlations between the perceived influence of law school on black jurists with their role perceptions shed little light on the larger issues of continuity and change. The results are even more mixed and baffling than those found under socioeconomic origins. For example, there is no difference between the perception of racial progress and the varying degrees of influence ascribed to law school. There are only minor, even fractional, differences between those who said that law school was important on their thinking and those who said it was not at all important. Over half (55 percent) of the judges rating their professional training highly noted that there had been substantial race progress in the past two decades, but the same percentage who were mildly enthusiastic about law school influence agreed. Even more indicative of the lack of clarity on this measure of association, 52 percent of the arbiters who thought their legal training was not a salient factor on their lives and careers declared that there had been great race advancement. The degrees of weight ascribed to professional training and of perceptions of racial achievement were too evenly distributed to yield any appreciative strength (Kendall's Tau c = .01) or an acceptable significance (p = .42). The finding here seemingly comports with Lortie's conclusion.

Neither were there significant relationships found between degrees of law school influence and of perceptions of racism in community courts (p = .33 and Kendall's Tau b = .02). Those judges who declared that law school was not important were much more likely to say that race bias was high in their local court systems (25 percent) than their cohorts who said it was mildly and very meaningful (13 percent and 14 percent, respectively). Superficially, these percentages would seem to contrast greatly. But, to further stir the mix, approximately the same percentage (40 percent) of each category of law school evaluators marked racism as low, with the remainder describing it as moderate. One must pause before reaching any conclusion or before offering any explanation.

The interdependence of law school evaluation and a willingness to protect the rights of blacks is the next order of business. When these two factors were correlated, a clear pattern emerged but was not significant (p = .10). Those who thought law school was not important were evenly divided on the question of whether black judges should take a special protective view. Those who said professional school was moderately important were most likely to agree that black judges should take such a position (53 percent); and those who said it was very important were least likely to do so (45 percent). This pattern seems to indicate that law school does play some part in the black judge's view of his role, especially as it relates to blacks. Our analysis of the influence of Howard Law suggested as much. It possibly even indicates that law school is a conservative influence on the attitudes of some judges. But given the various law school experiences of these judges, this correlation is not illuminating.

The correlations of law school influence may obscure more than they clarify, but they definitely do not suggest that a legal educaiton is a conservative influence on students. For example, those black judges who noted that their professional training was important are most likely to opt for judicial innovation (44 percent). And those who said it was not important are most likely to favor the cautious position of applying the law (37 percent), though over 42 percent of them also believed in enacting new laws. Two fifths of the moderate evaluators noted the urge of striking new legal directions, while 44 percent straddle the line between employing precedents and innovating. The moderate assessors are also least likely to affirm the conservative stance of applying settled doctrine (17 percent versus 20 percent of "very important" versus 37 percent of "not important"). These findings seem to fly in the face of the pattern ascertained on the issue of special black protection, but they are insignificant (p = .20) since only a few percentage points differentiate most positions. Yet the supposedly conservative influence of the legal discipline is again questioned. If law is a profession of traditions and law school is the initial agent of such socialization, one could expect to uncover significant and strong associations between law school importance and judicial innovation. Nothing of the sort has been discerned thus far.

Furthermore, the findings on the persuasive powers of a legal education and attitudes toward judicial policymaking may completely disabuse any lingering notions about the inculcation of traditional values while still a law student. The relationship discovered is highly significant, with less than a 2 to 100 change of sampling error. While over a quarter (27 percent) of the black judges who remarked that their professional education was a very important influence believed that judges should make substantial public policy, only a tenth of this group note that there should be no bench-made programs. Yet, of those who said that law school was not important, over 40 percent advocated the "conservative" position of no judicially fashioned policy. To add further confusion, over a quarter (26 percent) of those who said "not important" thought that judges should substantially mold public programs. Moreover, the relationship is a significant one, though of only moderate strength (Kendall's Tau b = .12). The two fifths of "not importants" who would advise formulating no bench policy is the apparent source of this significance.

The judges who had temperate assessments of professional school were least likely to favor great exertions by members of the judiciary (21 percent) and also least likely to vote for no effort at all (9 percent). Seven tenths of these moderate evaluators adopted the centrist position of some court-fashioned policy, compared to 62 percent of high and 32 percent of low school assessors.

Overall, these correlations are so bereft of any consistent pattern that it is impossible to state the influence of law school on judicial role perceptions. While the statistically unacceptable finding on the issue of special black protection might indicate the conservative powers of a legal education, the acceptable finding on judicial policymaking would more strongly suggest the opposite. Thus, we must look elsewhere.

Since law school influence is not the source of the role perceptions or "conservatism" of black judges, possibly the academic class rank of the respondents can solve the puzzle. After all, one of the quips of the legal profession is that the *A* students become professors, the *B* students become judges, and the *C* students become lawyers. While our examination of the academic performance of the members of the black bench cannot be this precise, we can gauge their views against their self-described class ranking.

Removing the few respondents who were in the bottom third of their classes and those few who were uncertain of their ranking for statistical purposes, we find no evidence that the highly ranked law graduates were inculcated with any more traditional notions of adjudicating than their lesser ranked brethren. For instance, on the controversial item of a special protective role for black litigants, 45 percent of the law graduates in the top-third of their classes affirmed this function, while the remainder dissented. Yet 56 percent of the middle-third students replied "yes" to this role for the black judge. But the association is not significant (p = .29; phi = .10).

Looking at the issue of judicial activity, the black judges who graduated in the middle-third of their classes were slightly more inclined to favor applying the law (21 percent) but also more notable for choosing to innovate (46 percent) than those in the upper-third of the academic ratings (18 percent for applying the law and 41 percent for bench intervention). Even given the pattern discerned, the differences are not major and the significance is not acceptable (p = .40).

The same pattern is unveiled on the question of judicial policymaking. Those judges in the academic middle of their law school class were slightly more marked in approving substantial moves to mold public policy than their top-ranking cohorts (28 percent and 24 percent, respectively). Nevertheless, these middle-ranked graduates were slightly more agreeable to no such exertions than their higher-graded colleagues (14 percent versus 12 percent), with all others voting for the moderate stance of some attempt. As with the previous two associations, this one is not significant (p = .38).

Thus the outside possibility that class rankings were a reflection of the indoctrination of legal traditions also proves to be a false key. Given the findings on both law school influence and class rank, it is possible to conclude, as did one judge: law school only reenforces previous inclinations. Since on-the-job training has been found to be an important shaper of professional values, we now investigate the law practices of black judges in search of the precise influences of race and robe on their judicial beliefs.

LAW PRACTICE

Lortie has concluded that since law school does not influence role perception, it is plausible that the type of law practice exerts a greater influence on professional socialization and thus on judges' images of their roles.

In correlating law practice with selected dependent variables, we will focus upon those black judges whose principal prebench careers were in private practice and in the offices of the prosecutor. Since many respondents were in other job categories and have been removed from the succeeding correlations, the numbers of judges vary, ranging from 116 to 137. We focus on private practitioners and prosecutors for the sake of clarity and contrast. Though the category of private practice masks a variety of clienteles and subject-matter specializations, many private practitioners defended criminal defendants. Counselors for the state, on the other hand, were obligated to prosecute such defendants.

The utility of this division of private practitioners and prosecutors becomes obvious on the first correlation. Black judges who spent their careers in the prosecutor's office are more likely than other respondents to think that there has been very much racial progress in the last two decades. Over 60 percent of them take this position, whereas their peers in private practice are almost evenly divided between perceiving very much and some/no race advancement (51 percent and 49 percent, respectively). This seeming optimism by careerists from the office of the district attorney has to be discounted, however, because the significance level (p = .10) is double the acceptable standard.

Yet the theme of optimism for prosecutorial careerists is not deceptive; it is reflected in the next test for association as well. This configuration, moreover, has the added fillip of being highly significant (only a 2 of 1,000-chance for sampling error). Though low, the relationships are among the strongest of any uncovered thus far (Kendall's Tau c = .17). There is a connection between career position and views of level of race bias in their community courts as defined by these black judges. For instance, two thirds of those who spent their careers in private practice believed that racism is high or moderate. Only two fifths of the former state counselors agreed. On the other side of the continuum, 60 percent of the black judges coming from the office of the district attorney noted judicial discrimination by race to be low, which contrasts markedly with former private lawyers—only a third concurred. Though one of our respondents, a former prosecutor, has publicly documented racial discrimination in his old office, the majority of his brethren have not reached a similar conclusion. For this majority to find otherwise may seem to them akin to indicting themselves and/or their legal colleagues.

When these black judges were asked if black judges should use their powers with a special view toward protecting the rights of blacks, we again find a positive relationship with career positions though neither significance (p = .05) nor strength (Cramer's V = .10) are at the levels of the previous correlation. While those respondents coming from private practice were evenly split on the question of black protection, over three fifths (63 percent) of their peers with prosecutorial careers replied negatively to this query. From this finding, we may tentatively conclude that most of the black judges who were professional prosecutors are unlikely to manifest a special sensitivity to race while on the bench. In contrast to other respondents who gave such answers as "yes and to all others" to the issue of black protection, a substantial percentage of former prosecutors completely disavowed this notion. Whether the obligation to prosecute disposes them to such a position cannot be definitively answered in this study.

If career prosecutors are viewed as proponents of judicial restraint, the next correlation could provide further substantiation for this proposition. Over a quarter (26 percent) of the black judges who had been career district attorneys believed that members of the judiciary should apply the law. But only 16 percent from private practice took this stance of judicial restraint. While somewhat less than half (46 percent) of the jurists from private practice thought that judges should be legal innovators, slightly more than a third (35 percent) of the former prosecutors opted for this activist function. And there is only a marginal difference between the two groups favoring the centrist posture of "in-between"— 38 percent of private barristers and 39 percent of former prosecutors. Overall, respondents who spent their careers in the private practice of law tended to believe in innovation, while former district attorneys were more nearly distributed between applying the law and innovating. The relationship between career jobs and views of judicial activism is discernible but not statistically significant (p = .07).

In contrast, the relationship between previous career and views of judicial policymaking is highly significant, with a 7 of 1,000-probability of sampling error. The observed pattern is one of our stronger ones (Kendall's Tau c = .15). Again, judges who spent their careers in the prosecutor's office are more likely to favor judicial restraint than those who were in private practice. For example, almost 30 percent of the black judges with careers in the private sector thought that judges should substantially attempt to make public policy, while only a tenth (11 percent) of the former career prosecutors favored such a course of action. On the other hand, approximately a tenth (12 percent) of the career private practitioners opted for no judicial policymaking, but a fifth (22 percent) of the career prosecutors agreed with this aspect of judicial restraint. It may be misleading, however, to characterize former career prosecutors as believers in bench restraint. After all, two thirds favored some judicial policymaking; and 60 percent of the former career private practitioners took the same view. Possibly these advocates of the middle position believe that, in deciding cases and issues, a judge unavoidably makes public policy.

The correlations of law school influence and class rank and judicial role perceptions yielded no consistent pattern, and we may conclude that law schools are not the ideological shapers that many have spposed. A legal education may do nothing more than provide convenient tools to accompany existing ideologies. The type of legal career before becoming judges was clearly more important on professional self-images than were law schools. In comparing private practitioners and prosecutors, a consistent and in some cases significant pattern emerged in which former career prosecutors were more inclined to favor judicial restraint and less inclined to support a special view of protecting black litigants. Overall, these findings agree with earlier ones; law practice is a greater professional socializing agent than law school.

Heeding Alfred North-Whitehead's admonition against one factor analysis, we continue our search for other influences on the role perceptions of black judges, turning now to judicial recruitment.

Chapter 10
Politics
and Judicial Attitudes

Human beings are the essential ingredient of politics. Though institutional structures and prescriptive regulations set the limits of political interplay, at least in stable regimes, they alone cannot account for the variety of governmental processes and policies. Human beings, individually and collectively, are the lifeblood of government, while organizations and rules are merely the framework for this field of social interaction. Thus, we now focus on the extrainstitutional politics of black judges, ranging from their judicial recruitment to their civil rights activity before ascending the bench. These factors may be found to have an affect on the judicial attitudes of our respondents.

In the dizzying welter of percentages and statistics discussed thus far, it may be wise to reiterate our goal. We seek to delineate as precisely as possible the forces, including race and judicial role, that have shaped the thinking of black judges.

JUDICIAL RECRUITMENT

Judgeships are choice patronage plums for political organizations. Dispensation of such positions rewards the party faithful, provides incentives for lower level political workers, installs allies in powerful slots on the bench, and curries favor with particular blocs of voters. These objectives are realized through the appointment process which, as noted in chapter 5, operates both for appointive and elective judgeships. Over three quarters of black judges, for instance, were initially appointed to their benches, though less than half sit on courts officially designated as appointive. Though this is not an example of the appointment process that they envision, the American Bar Association, newspapers, and other interested parties throughout the country, have been calling for a wholly appointed judiciary. One black judge, in an interview, strongly criticized this "reform" measure as an attempt to insure black underrepresentation on the judiciary, now that Afro-Americans are approaching majority status in many cities. Among the many themes implicit in his criticism is the idea that an elective bench would insure more black judges and greater judicial sensitivity to the black plight. This is a questionable idea. Some studies have found that methods of judicial recruitment do not seem to make any difference in the ideological distribution of judges. But Ish had findings that disputed this assertion; trial jurists who were elected to the bench were less likely to favor judicial restraint. The issue of whether method of recruitment influences judicial role perception is still debatable. This examination of black judges should provide further evidence.

Before advancing to the test of association, a note of explanation is advisable. Since we have already seen how the elective positions have become in fact appointive ones, the initial method of entry, elected or appointed, is used. Thus, the number of respondents will vary from a low of 132 to a high of 179, depending on the relationships examined. Our investigation of actual recruitment allows us to speculate on the motives of the appointing officer. Does he usually choose candidates "who are safe on the issues" for the judiciary? On the other side, such an inspection will provide light on the issue of whether an elected bench is more sensitive to the wishes of an increasingly black electorate than an appointed one. The stakes in these issues appear to be high because they lie at the heart of democratic theory.

In the first correlation, we find no evidence that the method of initial judicial recruitment shapes the perceptions of racial progress. These black judges, both elected and appointed, were almost evenly divided. Slightly over half of each group believed that there has been substantial racial progress during the past twenty years—52 percent of elected and 54 percent of appointed jurists. The remainder discerned only some or no racial improvement. This even split accounts for the level of significance ($p = .39$) being almost eight times the acceptable one, and the test of association is so minuscule (.01) as to indicate no relationship whatever between the two variables.

When examining their views of racism in court, we discover a slightly greater percentage of the elected judges than the appointed ones claiming court discrimination to be high in their community (17 percent compared to 14 percent). However, a much greater percentage also remarked that such bias was low (51 percent), with almost a third (32 percent) spying moderate judicial dislike of blacks. Only 35 percent of the appointed judges described court racism as low, and half said it was moderate. While there is a clear pattern between method of recruitment and views of judicial racism, the statistical significance ($p = .06$) is a fraction above the acceptable level. Furthermore, this correlation does not indicate that elected judges will be more sensitive than appointed ones in their treatment of black litigants. It may be that elected black jurists cite their own election as evidence that community racism is low.

When black members of the bench are asked about their judicial obligations to blacks, no distinct difference is discovered between those who were appointed and those who were elected to their posts. In both groups, slightly over half replied that black judges should not exercise their powers with a special view toward protecting the rights of fellow race-members who appear before the bench; 53 percent of elected and 52 percent of appointed respondents voted against this stance. Here again, the statistical significance is very high (p = .46), and the measure of strength is almost invisible (Cramer's V = .005).

When probed as to their view of judicial activism, the pattern seen on court racism resurfaces. Approximately a quarter (24 percent) of elected black jurists believed that judges should apply the law, leaving innovation to the legislatures. A fifth (19 percent) of their appointed brethren agreed with this role of restraint. Nevertheless, on the other extreme, the appointed members of the black bench were slightly more inclined to favor judicial invention (43 percent contrasted with 38 percent of elected ones). Almost equal percentages of appointed and elected respondents embraced the moderate duty of "in-between"—38 percent for each. While there is a pattern, there is no significant interrelationship between method of recruitment and perceptions of judicial activism (p = .18). Once, when told of the brilliant men surrounding President Kennedy, a troubled Sam Rayburn, Speaker of the House of Representatives, replied that, while they were good boys, he regretted that not one of them had ever run for sheriff. In that same vein, the election process may have chastened these elected black judges against much judicial activity.

If they were tempered by their election campaign, however, it was not appreciably more than their appointed colleagues. When probed as to what extent judges should shape public policy, approximately a quarter of the appointed and elected black bench members (25 percent and 23 percent, respectively) responded "substantial." While slightly more of the elected members maintained that judges should not fashion public programs (18 percent versus 13 percent), three fifths of each said they should make some attempt (59 percent for elected and 62 percent for appointed jurists).

Contrary to expectations, elected black judges are not more racially sensitive or judicially active in their attitudes than their appointed counterparts. In fact, they may be less sensitive, at least while on the bench. Elected bench members even appear to be slightly more inclined to agree with judicial restraint than appointed ones.

Moreover, assuming that the black voter is more important to elected than appointed black arbiters, there is evidence that he too is not any more influential on their attitudes than other recruitment factor. For example, those judges who noted the weight of black voters in their move to the bench were evenly split on the issue of a special protective role of blacks coming into their courts. Those who esteemed the minority electorate were less marked in choosing to innovate (33 percent) than either elected (38 percent) or appointed (43 percent) bench members. They were however more dominant (48 percent) in the middle stance between repeating legal precedents and inventing new doctrine than either elected or appointed jurists (38 percent for each).

The evidence mounts even more when comparing judges emphasizing the black vote with those underlining the significance of professional standing and political party in their judicial anointment. When interrogated as to what extent judges should shape policy, those citing the black vote were fractionally more likely to veto any such effort than the other citators (13 percent versus 11 percent for party and 12 percent for professional virtue). While 23 percent endorsed great exertions to shape policy from the bench, 24 percent of party and 21 percent of professional standing concurred. The influence of the black population on the bench attitudes of Afro-American judges is no greater than that of other, more frequently commended recruitment causes.

We must conclude that method of recruitment and even salient associated factors do not influence judicial role beliefs. Both judicial recruitment and related constituents may be part of those background variables that mask a variety of local political cultures. In the aggregate, this variety may obscure any relationship between appointments and elections and judicial role perceptions. All of our findings and conclusions are of course hampered by a lack of significance.

Nevertheless, the very lack of a significant interplay between these variables is itself noteworthy. Elected judges may indeed have been chastened by their campaigns for office. In addition, almost all of them preside in jurisdictions that contain substantial numbers, even majorities, of white voters. They appear to be the middle-of-the-road types who have historically received the blessings of the American voter. Furthermore, many of the elected respondents had been party activists and had been "slated" by their party chieftains to run for the bench. This too hampered the effort to have blacks on the bench who were especially sensitive to black social and economic conditions. In sum, if the executive officer appointed moderate blacks, a safe assumption, his care was apparently matched by other actors in the political system, be they party officers or voters.

POLITICAL PARTY

For many political elites, party affiliation is accepted as a predictor, even if imprecise, of the origins, attitudes, and behavior of party adherents. Generally speaking, Democrats tend to be from the lower-middle and working classes and from minority groups, and to be "liberal" on economic, social, and political issues. The obverse characterizes members of the Republican party. The "liberalism" of Democrats and the "conservatism" of Republicans are reflections of their attitudes on the power of the government. Supporters of the party of

Jefferson-Jackson advocate governmental action to protect and enhance the opportunities of the disadvantaged. On the other side, the champions of the party of Lincoln-Coolidge stress restricted interference of the political system in economic and social spheres.

These findings on the relationship between party and attitudes are valid not only for the mass membership but especially for political leaders. Within leadership groups, party is also a salient factor for judges. Before recruitment to the bench, judges have often been politically active, and party plays a role in their selection to the judiciary. It is probable that being more active, they develop a greater knowledge and belief in party doctrine. Party has been shown to be a predictor of attitudes and behavior at judicial levels of government. Political affiliations have been related to the decisions in economic, criminal, civil liberties, and other types of cases in both federal and state courts. Finally, to add the proverbial icing to the cake, it should be noted that black Americans and black elected officials are likely to be both more Democratic and more liberal than the general population.

Given the well-documented relationship between party and ideology, the findings here on the relationship of party with the role perception of black judges are not surprising. Black Democratic judges are more likely to take an activist stance on role perception questions than their black Republican brethren. Not all correlations were statistically significant, but the party pattern is still evident. For instance, the Republican respondents were more prone than Democrats to think that there had been an appreciable degree of improvement in race relations in the past two decades. Three fifths of the followers of Lincoln's party said as much, though only 54 percent of the Jeffersonians did. In addition, the remaining two fifths of the GOP members discerned some or no forward movement in race relations in the country, with 46 percent of the opposing party spying the same degree of achievement. While the party configuration appears to be fairly distinct, it must be discounted because of the lack of statistical significance (p = .14).

The political party differentials are again evident when correlating the party factor with perceived court racism. Moreover, this correlation is statistically significant (p = .03), though of weak strength (Kendall's Tau c = .10). While 15 percent of the black Democratic judges viewed race bias in their community judiciary as high, only 9 percent of their Republican opposites affirmed that view. But almost half (49 percent) of the Republicans sighted such discrimination as low, with less than 38 percent of Democrats concurring. Furthermore, as half (47 percent) of the Jefferson party members were beholding bench bias as moderate, their opponents in the party of Lincoln were somewhat reluctant to agree (42 percent).

Addressing party affiliations and functions of judicial black protection, we again find a significant association (p =.05), but also again uncover a measure of limited strength (Cramer's V = .09). When asked if black judges should exercise their powers with special emphasis on protecting the rights of blacks, the Democratic judges split almost evenly on this measure of race duty (49 percent for and 51 percent against). Yet over three fifths (61 percent) of the adherents of the Lincoln camp maintained that members of the black judiciary should disavow such a stance, even though 39 percent of their bedfellows assented to this extraordinary posture. Given the Republican tendency to think that the country has made substantial racial progress and that racism is low in their community courts, the finding on this last question is not too surprising. In effect, these black Republican judges appear to be moderate in their perceptions of their judicial roles, even as it relates to their fellow blacks. And this is so even though they were among the overwhelming majority of respondents who noted that the country is still far from achieving racial equality. They may be among those old-fashioned advocates of equality who believe that race discrimination, must be erased immediately. In their view, the concept of evenhandedness under the law does not recognize race.

Correlating party with judicial activity, the party distinctiveness remains, though statistical significance evaporates (p = .12). The Republican predilection for limited government extends to the judiciary; the general activism of Democrats includes the bench. While slightly over two fifths (41 percent) of the black Democratic judges believed in judicial innovation, an almost equal percentage (39 percent) of GOP jurists took this same stance. But party differences are most exposed on the other end of bench functions. For instance, though slightly less than 18 percent of the Democrats encouraged applying the law, the position of restraint, over 28 percent of the Republicans, approved of this limited view. The remaining partisans flocked to the middle of the road—41 percent of Democrats and 33 percent of Republicans chose "in-between."

Moreover, there are no strong, meaningful associations uncovered between party affiliations and attitudes toward judicial policymaking (p = .14), even though the party cleavage continues. Black judicial Republicans were somewhat less marked than their Democratic counterparts to think that judges should substantially attempt to participate in shaping public programs (21 percent for GOP and 25 percent for Democrats). Conversely, they were somewhat more prone to approve of the stance that judges should not make any move to mold governmental output (18 percent for Republican judges versus 13 percent for Democratic ones). It is curious that 62 percent of each group of partisans would affirm the pose that members of the judiciary should shape some public policy. This sizable percentage indicates that black judges from both parties believe in some judicial activism. A Republican interviewee thought judges "should exercise the moral strength of their positions to influence policy for the good of society." He and others recalled their policy decision in juvenile, penal, and law enforcement areas. One of his Democratic neighbors maintained judicial policymaking is important because blacks "need public support." He boasted,

It was my decision that was affirmed by the Supreme Court that established the famous Community Legal Services in America...(It was the) greatest opinion that was given to help the minorities, the underprivileged in America, white, black...

The decision to formulate at least some public policy is anchored in race consciousness and was taught by the Warren Court. One black Republican cited the Supreme Court's decision in *Brown* v. *Board of Education:* "If there was ever a policy decision, in the finest sense of policy...that was one." While lower courts operate within a narrower policymaking framework than the nation's highest tribunal, many cases must be decided daily. "And whichever way you decide, it is going to affect the course of human conduct."

In general, a consistent though weak pattern is found when examining the influence of party affiliation upon the role perceptions of black judges. There are slight differences in self-images between black Republican and Democratic judges. The consistent pattern uncovered is of Republican moderateness and Democratic activism.

Many observers have commented in recent years that the two major American parties have become fuzzy in their differences on current issues, even though Republicans generally encourage limited governmental exertions and Democrats on the whole approve of great efforts by the political system. The findings on the association of political party membership with the role attitudes of black judges confirm these observations. There is a hazy issue distinction between the two partisan groups of Afro-American jurists. A party schism emerges, but it is bland and statistically insignificant.

POLITICAL AND JUDICIAL IDEOLOGIES

Since Democratic party members are seen as more liberal than their Republican cohorts, both on and off the bench, political ideology should be examined as an influence on judicial role perceptions. There are grounds for assuming that ideology plays an equal, if not greater, role than party in attitudes and behavior. Ish found that ideology was related to the role attitudes of local trial judges. Wold and Sheldon Goldman, furthermore, revealed the interplay of ideology and the behavior of state and federal appellate benches. Thus, it should be examined directly, and not inferentially by political party affiliation. This examination of political ideology will focus on liberals and moderates, because only a few black jurists described themselves as conservatives.

Approximately the same percentage of self-described liberals as moderates thought that substantial racial progress had been achieved in the last twenty years (52 percent versus 54 percent, respectively). This possibly indicates that some factor other than ideology determines or shapes estimates of racial progress, since the measure of significance is highly unacceptable (p = .40).

This fairly equitable distribution of liberals and moderates is broken on the question of racism in their local systems, in which the liberals were more prone to characterize it as high (17 percent) than the moderates were (13 percent). The centrists judges tended to regard bench bias as low (43 percent), though somewhat over a third of the left-leaning brothers agreed (35 percent). Approximately equal percentages of each group of ideologists perceived it to be mild (54 percent of moderates and 48 percent of progressives). While there is a pattern, it is not a significant one (p = .09).

The ideological division suggested on court racism becomes a stronger configuration on the question of a black protective function by the black bench members (Cramer's V = .22). The test for significance yields a very impressive .0000. The black liberal jurists was much more likely to answer affirmatively that Afro-American judicial officers should be especially disposed to protecting the rights of blacks (58 percent) than those who called themselves moderate in outlook (35 percent). Almost two thirds (65 percent) of the middle-of-the-road judges were adamant in their opposition to this special duty, though just two fifths (42 percent) of the left-wing respondents concurred. This ideological break is clear-cut, and it is much greater than that found under the party factor. The strength of the association between ideology and black protection is the strongest discovered thus far. It may be that race sensitivity underlies more the ideology of the liberal black jurist than of his moderate colleague.

The distinctive rupture found on black protection is maintained on the questions of the general judicial role, and this difference is also greater than that found under the party variable. This very probably indicates that political ideology is a greater predictor than party of the role attitudes of these black judges. When probed, for example, as to judicial lawmaking, the liberal respondents were much more likely to encourage bench innovation than the moderate ones. Slightly less than half (49 percent) of the self-described leftist arbiters favored legal changes flowing from the judiciary, and slightly less than a third (33 percent) of the middle-of-the-road subjects approved. Moving to the other end of the continuum of judicial functions, approximately a fifth of each group of ideologists affirmed the "conservative" posture of merely applying the law—21 percent of moderates and 18 percent of liberals. However, the centrists have described themselves aptly since they dominate the middling position of "in-between." Almost half of them embraced this function, though only a third of the champions of progressivism did. This correlation of political ideology with judicial activism is significant (p = .01), but of only mild strength (Kendall's Tau c = .13).

However, matching political beliefs with views of judicial policymaking provides more impressive results. The significance of the relationship is very high (p = .0003), and even the strength of the association is improved (Kendall's Tau c = .19). When questioned as to what extent judicial officers should attempt to fashion public policies, over 30 percent of the black liberal judges advocated substantial judicial motion, while only 11 percent of the centrists did likewise. Conversely, only a tenth of the progressives noted that judges should not make programs from the bench, while 18 percent of the moderates affirmed this decision. On this test also, the moderates overwhelmingly straddled the middle slot. Seven out of ten approved "some" effort to devise policy from the bench, while slightly less than six out of ten of the left-leaning respondents followed this example.

While political ideology is neither related to perceptions of racial progress or of court racism, it is significantly connected to the specific perceptions of judicial role. This political mind-set correlates more strongly with variables of self-image than does party. In general, politically liberal black judges are more prone to favor judicial activism and black protection, than their politically moderate colleagues.

Since political ideology has been found to be consistently related to the role perceptions of members of the Afro-American bench, it may be worthwhile to probe judicial ideology. This is especially so since we have already seen a softening of the ideological tendencies of black judges after they ascended to the judiciary. Though liberalism dominates both political and judicial fields, moderatism enjoyed a noticeable surge as the judges shifted from their political to judicial mind-sets. This aroused suspicions that the traditional judicial role had silently crept into the beliefs of the respondents. An investigation of this phenomenon can thus clarify that question, at least in part.

Focusing on the perceptions of racial progress, a pattern is revealed that is almost identical to that uncovered on political ideology. Approximately half of both judicial liberals and moderates spied substantial improvement in race relations (51 percent and 55 percent, respectively). The remainder were in the collapsed category of some or no race enhancement. As with political ideology, this association yielded neither significance (p = .28) nor strength (Kendall's Tau b = .05). The findings on both political and judicial belief systems may suggest that views of race progress are not grounded in ideology, at least not for these respondents.

However, the configuration that materializes on estimates of judicial racism is a sharp one. Though the significance is fractionally unacceptable (p = .06) and the relationship is comparatively soft (Kendall's Tau c = .13) judicial liberals discerned greater race bias then their moderate benchmates. For instance, over 18 percent of the progressives but less than 8 percent of the middle-liners described court discrimination as high. While equal proportions of each assessed bench bias as mild (47 percent liberals and 49 percent moderates), over two fifths (43 percent) of the centrists believed it to be low compared to a bit over a third (34 percent) of the progressives who nodded in accord. This pattern is almost perfectly parallel to that seen with political ideology and court racism.

The judicial ideological schism is maintained on the issue of a special protective role but significance (p = .17) is also above the acceptable standard and the strength is still vapid (phi = .13). These measurements are especially disturbing since the cleavage is so abrupt. Almost three fifths (58 percent) of liberal judges vowed a special judicial function of guarding the rights of Afro-Americans, though only 45 percent of the moderate bench members took the same oath. Those declaring negatively to this extraordinary pledge were the remainders—42 percent liberals and 55 percent moderates. Judicial ideology is apparently no more mingled in the bench attitudes than the political mind-sets were. Indeed, they may be less related, since the correlation of political ideology with this special role had both great significance and a measure of strength.

However, looking at the associations revealed on judicial activity, we find the most potency laid bare yet (Kendall's Tau c = .35) and a level of significance that ranks with the best previously found (p = .0000). The measurements are not deceptive, though we may have run into the problem of phrasing the same question in two different ways. But if this were so, the proportion of strength would be even greater than seen here.

Only one fifth (21 percent) of the moderates favored judicial innovation, but over half (54 percent) of the judicial liberals marked it. Exactly half of the centrists, and a third of their leftward fellow judges agreed to "in-between." Moreover, almost 30 percent of the middle-of-the-road judges versus 13 percent of the progressive ones disavowed such bench activity by choosing to apply the law.

The intimate interplay of judicial ideology with judicial activity is not a happenstance. This can be ascertained in correlating judicial belief systems with bench policymaking. Here again, there is significance (p = .01) and a relationship of mild strength (Kendall's Tau c = .17). When interrogated as to the desired degree of bench participation in policy areas, almost a third (32 percent) of the judicial liberals recommended great exertions by the judiciary; yet only 14 percent of moderate judicial officers asserted such a claim. As found in political beliefs, the moderates were straddling the middle ground. Almost three quarters (73 percent) opted for some bench participation in popular programs, with 57 percent of their progressive colleagues agreeing. Both groups were reluctant to disavow any involvement in policy-making, though moderates were more likely to do so than judicial liberals (14 percent versus 11 percent).

Overall, judicial ideology is an influence in the bench beliefs of black judges, but it is not the great determinator that it was suspected to be. While the power of judicial ideology and judicial activity was the greatest by far yet discovered, political ideology was more consistently strong and meaningful in its association with the job attitudes of black judges. The usefulness of judicial belief systems was especialy notable for their lack of a certifiable sway on the question of a special protective role for the black bench. This suggests that the robe of the black judge has not overwhelmed his sensitivity to race, even if it has moderated views of court duty. Since ideology and race are intimately connected, civil rights activity is a likely subject to further clarify the questions surrounding the race and robe of black judges.

RACE CONSCIOUSNESS

Given the long history of turbulent, abusive racial relations in this country, the relevance of race as a factor influencing the role perceptions of black judges cannot be doubted. Indeed, we have already found that race was a factor in their backgrounds, socialization, and judicial recruitment.

The movement for racial equality in the American nation was primarily a propagandistic and legal one. Since most of these judges were practicing attorneys at the height of the legalistic phase of the civil rights movement, their activity in the fight for civil rights is studied as a possible determinant of their self-images as judges. We assume that degrees of civil rights activism can be equated with degrees of race consciousness.

In these correlations, a strong and almost perfect relationship exists between civil rights activity and perceptions of judicial duty. The patterns on civil rights, in fact, are the only consistently significant ones found. Black judges who were very active in the civil rights struggle are much more likely to favor judicial activism; those who were less active are correspondingly less inclined to approve such bench activity.

The jurists who were greatly active in the fight for black equality were least likely to think the country has achieved substantial racial progress in the last twenty years. Less than half (47 percent) noted very much advancement. Meanwhile, the moderate race activists were more prone to assess a great forward movement in race harmony (55 percent). And those nonactivist blacks were most favorable in their measurements—seven out of ten claimed that there had been much race progress. In other words, the more active the judges were in the civil rights movement, the less optimistic they were in gauging positive changes in race relations. Moreover, this relationship between degrees of civil rights participation and perceptions of racial progress is highly significant, with a 2 of 1,000-probability of sampling error, though not very strong (Kendall's Tau c = .14).

On the question of court racism, we again find significance (p = .03), even if it is not as great as that revealed on the previous correlation. The strength is also less (Kendall's Tau b = .10). Those black judges who were moderately or nonactive in the recent race struggle were more prone to think that racism in the courts of their community was low (46 percent each), whereas less than a third (31 percent) of the deeply involved race warriors agreed. The respondents who were very active notched judicial bias as high (16 percent) and moderate (53 percent). Yet, in a curious twist, the nonactives were also most notable in describing bench discrimination as high (18 percent), with 13 percent of the moderate participants sighting the same level. While 36 percent of the noncontributors perceived court racism as moderate, 42 percent of the limited contributors of the civil rights front gave the same estimate. Here again the race sensitivity of the judge shapes his evaluation of his world.

The saliency of race carries into the role perceptions of these black judges. While they may have collectively divided very sharply on the extraordinary function of a special protective role of Afro-Americans coming before their benches, those who were civil rights activists of the first rank were more disposed to consent to this duty than those who were less active in race matters. Indeed, there is a progressive pattern to the interplay of the two factors—60 percent of the very, 42 percent of the moderately, and 36 percent of the nonactives responded affirmatively to this question. On the other hand, the inactives were most adamant of all jurists in opposing this stance, with the proportions being the remainder of the positive answers. The relationship is a very significant one (p = .0001) and is among the strongest (Cramer's V = .20) found. Race consciousness does influence the role beliefs of black judges, especially on black issues.

Furthermore, regarding a general professional obligation, race sensitivity again surfaces as a force on members of the Afro-American bench. For example, civil rights activists were inclined to be judicial activists. Over half (51 percent) of the passionate champions of black rights among these respondents stood for judicial innovation, though only 35 percent of the mildly committed and 39 percent of those who played no part in the black movement agreed to this posture. At the other end of the spectrum, 28 percent of the inactives in race matters declared that the judge should apply the law, the "conservative" stand, followed in almost predictable order by 23 percent of the mild contributors and 14 percent of the intense contributors to the civil rights rebellion. However, a substantial portion of each group fell between the poles of judicial activity and restraint—35 percent of the enthusiastic, 42 percent of the quiet, and 33 percent of the apathetic civil rights actors embraced "in-between." Though this association is of moderate weight (Kendall's Tau b = .14), it is of great significance (p = .005).

When asked about judicial policymaking, the pattern just revealed continues. Moreover, it has improved strength (Kendall's Tau b = .20) and significance (p = .0001). Those Afro-American arbiters who were not active in the race struggle were opposed to activism from the bench. Almost 30 percent noted no attempt to fashion political policy from the judiciary, but less than 8 percent of the intensely active and 16 percent of the moderately active race workers concurred. At the opposite pole, almost a third of the militant civil rights proponents espoused great attempts to contribute to societal affairs by judges, though only 17 percent of the quiet fighters and 19 percent of the uninvolved followed this lead. Appropriately enough, the middle-range race combatants also selected the middle position on policy input. Exactly two thirds advocated some effort to judicially mold programs, while 59 percent of the staunch race defenders and 52 percent of the noncivil rights joiners acquiesced.

Yet civil rights involvement may not be the same for all participants. Since militant black organizations were notable for the urgency of their race objectives, an examination of judges who were members of the Congress of Racial Equality (CORE), the Southern Christian Leadership Conference (SCLC), and the Student Nonviolent Coordinating Committee (SNCC), could provide a more precise view of race sensitivity and civil rights participation than uncovered thus far. This is especially so when they are compared to judges who were not affiliated with these groups. Using the judicial policymaking question, because of its consistent strength and significance on almost all dimensions, interesting patterns are revealed but no certifiable association. For instance, black judges who joined militant black groups were more inclined to propose great judicial labor to participate in policy-shaping than nonjoiners. Almost 30 percent of the militant members approved of this court function, compared to 24 percent of the members of sedate black federations. The differences between the two camps are most evident at the other extreme. Over 16 percent of the nonmilitants but only 5 percent of the combatants encouraged no judge-made programs. The lack of significance ($p = .15$) may come from the large proportions occupying the middle option. Exactly two thirds of the former street marchers and 59 percent of the others chose some bench-move in policy matters. Thus, there are no appreciable differences apparent concerning the job beliefs of black judges by the types of civil rights alliances they joined.

Further indications of this are evident when comparing the former public demonstrators with members of the Urban League, whose tone and pitch are establishment-oriented. The street activists were more likely to advocate outstanding judicial input in policy than the boardroom urgers of the Urban League (29 percent versus 23 percent), and less disposed to deny all such participation (5 percent compared to 12 percent). However, members of both groups were concentrated in their adherence to some bench energy—67 percent for militants and 65 percent for Urban Leaguers. Race sensitivity transcends its outlet, at least for members of the Afro-American judiciary.

The saliency of politics quite probably causes the leader rather than the follower to develop a greater knowledge of, and belief in, party doctrine. This same phenomenon appears to have happened with civil rights activity. Those black judges who were civil rights activists reflected that activism in their role perceptions, just as those who were not formally active manifested their inactivity in their orientation toward their jobs. Sensitivity to civil rights activity prior to assuming judicial office influences role perception in general and protection of blacks in particular.

One interviewee who was not active in civil rights practically never thinks about race "unless somebody mentions it." However, judges who were active admit, as a senior judge put it, that "the obligation that I owe to my black people" shapes their perceptions of judicial duties. Many hoped it do so "unconsciously" or that it did not "show in court." Nevertheless, race underlies judicial role perceptions because

> If I'm black I'm more conscious of some of the shortcomings of...(and) more concerned about changes in the judicial system to take care of those injustices than I'm likely to be if I were white. That's all I'm saying.

More than social class, age, political party, and law school, race molds the self-images of Afro-American judges. The onus that white Americans have made of race pervades almost every aspect of the lives, careers, and attitudes of the respondents. Racial discrimination has provoked in black judges a seemingly ineradicable desire for changes in the status quo. This deep-seated desire may reshape the face of American society.

Chapter 11
Conclusions

Racism is a documented fact of American life. It pervades all levels of society, including the government. The judiciary has not been immuned to it; judges legitimated the racist practices of parts of the culture as well as perpetrated their own. Many persons assumed that the recent influx of Afro-American judges would lessen racial discrimination from the judiciary. This study sought to lay the groundwork for future impact assessments by ascertaining which factors, especially race or judicial role, might be most influential on the concept of official duties of black judges. Our task was twofold: (1) to provide a collective portrait of Afro-American jurists, particularly the influences of race and professionalism on their lives, careers, and self-images; and (2) by correlating selected background factors with their role perceptions, to gauge the power of race, robe, and other variables on their judicial attitudes. The effects of racial discrimination permeates almost every phase of the lives of these respondents. Furthermore, racial sensitivity was discovered to be among the elements affecting their images of judicial duty, along with age and political and judicial ideology. The restraint of their robes, underlined by its absence, was manifested by their apparent reluctance to practice fully the bench activity they preached and by the softening of their liberalism from political to judicial ideologies. But the abstract reins of their robes were overwhelmed by the concrete realities of race.

Focusing on particular background results, our conclusions are as follows:

(1) Over half of the black judicial officers were born in the South, though only 10 percent now sit there. The judges or their parents left that region because of the poor economic opportunities and blatant racism, and their concentration in northern urban areas reflects the large numbers of blacks in these jurisdictions.

(2) The age distribution of the respondents was similar to that found for other state trial judges. Over 70 percent were 45-65 years of age.

(3) Black jurists were more likely than white ones to come from working-class backgrounds. Over three fifths claimed to be from such homes, with a third citing middle-class status. Further, findings in this area seem to justify those students

who questioned the usefulness of the tripartite class distinction, especially as applied to blacks.

(4) While many of the judges changed from the religious affiliation of their parents, they tended to retain the political party allegiance bequeathed them. Their Republican party membership was greater than for the general black population, yet lagged behind the seven-tenths Democratic membership. While party allegiance showed the influence of inheritance, pragmatism, and ideology, race was also influential on party affiliations.

(5) Ideological alignment was comparable to that of party, with almost two thirds describing themselves as political liberals and less than a third claiming a moderate stance. This differed greatly from findings of nonblack trial and appellate judges. Ideology, in turn, was buttressed by race sensitivities. Liberals favored new approaches to problems, greater protection of civil liberties, and more governmental efforts to establish racial equality.

(6) The search for influences on political interest and activity yielded mixed results. The family was cited as the primary socializing agent in politics, which was not surprising since it also transmitted party affiliation. More specifically, over a quarter of the black judges in this study recalled that civil rights provoked their initial interest in political affairs. While a third remembered childhood as the first period of political interest, a quarter noted that it occurred in law practice. This latter result has been found by students of nonjudicial decision-makers, indicating that political socialization is a continuing process. Almost half of the black jurists used political parties as their vehicle for initial political activity. A number of reasons was cited for this choice: working for a particular candidate, being involved in business, and, more to our interest, improving the plight of blacks. This racial basis for political activity must have also motivated over a fifth of those who used the civil rights movement as their vehicle.

(7) The influence of family on legal interest was cited by a third, though a friend was noted by a quarter of the subjects. A quarter more chose diverse influences, with race being among them. For example, one pointed to the *Scottsboro* case as his provocation.

(8) On interest in a judgeship, the family influence was negligible. Half claimed their judicial interest came through their law practice, which substantially accounts for the nine tenths whose interest came after law school. This late ambition reflected the limited opportunities open to black Americans. Howard Law School graduated the greatest number of future black judges, again proving the contributions of black schools to improving the conditions of blacks. Over half of all the respondents thought law school was an important influence in their careers. Many Howard Law graduates felt that law school was important because of the civil rights activity of its faculty ands because it provided career opportunities. Finally, law school was not a conservative socializing agent because it only confirmed the students in their previous inclinations.

(9) Black lawyers here, as found in other studies, had difficulty establishing

their legal practice, with a quarter working in civil service positions after law school. The prosecutor's office was found to be an important launching position to the judiciary, with over 16 percent of respondents being career prosecutors.

(10) The legal fact of elective benches was proved to be only half true as less than a quarter of these judges were initially elected to their positions. This development of de facto appointive positions changed the nature of recruitment to the politics of the appointing officer. Professional standing and political party were recalled as intimately related to the appointing process. While less than a third of the respondents noted that black voters were factors in their judicial ascent, four fifths thought race was an important aid in their rise to the bench. In recruitment as in social background, race has been an omnipresent factor in the lives of black judges. The question inevitably arises as to what part race plays in their judicial role perceptions.

(11) Since the civil rights movement was predominantly a legalistic one for half a century, the civil rights activity of black jurists afforded a rough index of degrees of race consciousness. Almost 90 percent cited some activity in the movement for race equality, with nearly half listing themselves as very active. Substantial numbers were contributors, workers, and most important, officers in one or more of the civil rights organizations. Almost all of them confined their activities to the more moderate National Association for the Advancement of Colored People (NAACP) and the Urban League; very few were members of the more activist Students Nonviolent Coordinating Committee (SNCC) or Congress for Racial Equality. While very interested in racial concerns, black judges appear to be more reformers than revolutionaries. Even so, they thought the country had to achieve substantial progress before racial equality is realized, and that courts were vital in this process.

In an effort to ascertain the influences on the self-images of black judges, selected factors were correlated with role perceptions. We concluded that

(1) family status, religious affiliation, law school influence and rank, political party affiliation, and method of initial entry to the judiciary, had no affect on the role perceptions of Afro-American jurists. Other students had questioned the impact of these factors upon judicial attitudes; our findings tend to confirm their qualms.

(2) There was an inconsistent relationship between professional experiences before becoming judges and judicial role images. Black judges who spent their careers in the prosecutor's office were somewhat more likely than private practitioners to favor judicial restraint and less special protection for blacks, suggesting professional socialization in a government service.

(3) Political and judicial ideology, civil rights activity, and age, were related to the role attitudes of black judges. Liberal ideologists opted for positions of judicial activism, while moderates approved a view between activism and restraint. The ideology of the liberals evinced beliefs in greater governmental activity (hence their own leaning toward bench activism) and evinced more

sensitivity to racial equality. Civil rights activity provided the most consistently positive relationship with the bench attitudes of black judges. The respondents who were very active in civil rights were favorable to an energetic judiciary; the moderately active fighters for racial equality were less approving of this development. The relationship of civil rights and political ideology to attitudes were so close that they seem to flow from the same political concerns, at least for black judges. A mild surprise was the strong relationship between age and judicial orientations. Younger jurists seemed to be more impatient for bench activity, while those over age 60 were less impatient. This could be discounted as the energy of youths and the maturity of their seniors, except that the 50-59-age group also esteemed judicial activism. This relationship is not easily explained. Possibly, they were influenced by the activism of the 1960s, especially that of the United States Supreme Court. Our findings indicate that more research is needed in the area of age. While there was a relatively consistent relationship between four factors to judicial role perceptions, only one of the tests of association exhibited over a quarter percentage of strength on a scale of 0 to ±1. Thus, there may be other factors influencing attitudes not uncovered here.

Moreover, our inability to discover strong relationships has pointed out the usefulness of the biography. Once the staple of historians of various disciplines but now considered somewhat unfashionable, it can provide a more intimate connection between experience and beliefs than survey research can. The biographical problem of focusing on one or a few actors remains. But what it lacks in scope, it compensates in depth.

Furthermore, on the technical side, role theory is a useful concept for analyzing the interaction of black judges with other personalities. However, role will have to be precisely clarified if it is to be of practical research value. Role should be defined, as it has been in this study, as the dynamic interaction of a focal actor and his role partner that determines what his normatively expected duties are. This definition indicates that role is a set of evolving expectations that are shaped by the interplay of each group member's personality. Also, if role is to be an effective tool, the situation to which it applies must be clearly defined. The role of almost all judges can be determined by studying judges and the groups they regularly encounter in their jurisdictions.

Concern for the conditions of black Americans is so pervasive in the lives, careers, and attitudes of black judges that they seem to run the race argument into the ground. This sensitivity to race has apparently quashed the competition within these judges between two opposing sets of expectations, one held by professional associates and the other by racial cohorts. They are enjoined by professional expectations to be impartial, to adhere to established law, and to avoid the political controversies raging outside their chambers. These arbiters understand the need for stability and predictability in the law. The requirement that judges eschew even the appearance of partisanship is also accepted by them. The judiciary is the least powerful of the three branches of government and must rely upon the goodwill of the citizenry to preserve judicial influence. But black judges see fellow Afro-Americans as being powerless and impoverished. They realize that the judiciary has been a handmaiden to the racism that subjugates blacks. Even today this racism is evident in the court system. Blacks are more likely than whites to be arrested, charged high bail, found guilty, and sentenced to prison. On the civil side of the docket, racial discrimination takes a more covert form but is present nevertheless. Afro-American jurists appear to have resolved the quandary of continuing the prevailing judicial role of restraint or reshaping it. Provoked by racial experiences, black judges have adopted an attitude of judicial activism, though this appears to have been tempered by their expectations of disapproval from professional colleagues.

Their adoption of an attitude of activism leads to two questions. First, will black judges act on their beliefs? Uhlman has revealed that 16 black jurists in one community convicted and sentenced black and white defendants at approximately the same rate as their 79 white colleagues. However, this discovery is only the beginning of explanations of black judicial behavior. Among other things, as we have seen, race sensitivity varies among judges, even Afro-American ones. The degree of civil rights participation, age, ideology, and even law practice, have an impact on judicial attitudes. Thus, a large, finely tuned investigation of the Afro-American judiciary is needed to answer this question.

In addition, if these judges act on their aggressive instincts, what are the likely consequences for the judiciary and American race harmony? Even though American judges are generally restrained in their approach to adjudication, there is evidence that no uniform role structure controls them. The effects of the energetic ideas of black jurists will thus probably be determined by their personalities and values and by their major role partners, and by the facts, issues, and dispositions of the cases in question. Moreover, since only a small percentage of suits heard are ripe for innovation, the wrangles between activists and restraintists are likely to be underpublicized, low-key professional ones. This is even more so because members of the Afro-American bench are more reformers than revolutionaries. However, in those rare instances when the issues and dispositions of cases have enormous societal implications, the conflagration ensuing from this activism will likely flare among members of the profession and of the general public.

Indeed, the actions of a few black judges have already sparked great controversy, opprobrium, and in some cases, commendation from their communities. One Detroit respondent, aroused from his bed in the small hours of the morning, released on recognizance a host of individuals who had been arrested at a church meeting of a black separatist group. His rationale was that the police, responding to a reported sniping incident, would not have incarcerated a churchful of whites. The police, media, and other aggrieved parties howled in indignant disapproval. But months later, when the state supreme court affirmed his decision, he was hailed as having helped to prevent a riot.

Actions of comparable daring must flow from other black judges. They must not be cowered by the predictable negativism of some residents of their jurisdictions. The great racial disparities seen in arrest, detention, conviction, and imprisonment rates, demand examination, explanation, and remediation. Each judicial officer should approach his position, quietly or forthrightly, as a trust held for the black community as well as the majority white populace. He must be more than a model; he must be a mover. Solutions, farfetched or old-fashioned, must be urged on the bench, on the bar, and on the citizenry by black judges if the long-awaited goal of racial equality is to be realized. The judge knows the legal system better than the layman; he must provide the leadership in solving problems in this part of the social network. Sensitizing white judges and other court officers to race bias must be an ongoing concern. While most judges are confined by congested dockets to each case as it is brought before them, black ones must find the time, energy, and resources to speak conceptually on broad issues, especially those that impinge on black-white relations. The power of judges is finite, as all would agree, but their residual authority places them among the favored few of American society. They must not squander their opportunities to help right the wrongs of our times.

Yet this charge of duty is not limited to the judiciary. Other individuals must also make sacrifices and contributions. As the movement for race equality has entered a comparatively quiet phase, equal rights partisans must deepen their support for this age-old objective. The moral decay of idle hands that Booker T. Washington feared almost a century ago seems to have arrived in full force. Violent dispositions, petty thievery, widespread illegitimacy, denial of responsibility, shifting of blame, unwillingness to do quality work, searching for the easy way out, and finally endemic defeatism, are all threads in the rotten yarn of American race relations. These are the reasons why Washington and others sought to engage the numerous talents of black Americans. To do otherwise, then or now, is profligacy. Judges and ordinary citizens, and blacks and concerned whites, must all contribute, great and small, to the end of racial justice.

Appendix
Questionnaire for Black Judges

1. Birthplace ————————————————————————————
   If you grew up in some other community, which one? ——————

2. Age ——————————————————————————————————

3. Within your community, was your family considered

   working class ——————————————————————————————
   middle class ————————————————————————————————
   upper class —————————————————————————————————

4. What was the extent of your parents' formal education?

	father	mother

   grade school ————————————————————————————————
   high school —————————————————————————————————
   college ——————————————————————————————————————

5. What was your parents' religious affiliation? And what is your religious affiliation?

	your parents'	yours

   Catholic ————————————————————————————————————
   Protestant
     Baptist ——————————————————————————————————————
     Methodist ———————————————————————————————————
     Presbyterian ————————————————————————————————

Episcopalian _____

Other _____

Jewish _____

None _____

6. What was your father's occupation? _____

   What was your mother's occupation, if any? _____

7. Which political party did your parents favor?

   Democrat _____

   Republican _____

   Other _____

8. How politically active were your parents? (Check where applicable)

   a. voted _____

   b. members of political party _____

   c. members of nonpartisan political organization (e.g., NAACP or CORE)
   _____

   d. campaign worker _____

   e. campaign contributor _____

   f. ran for political office (what was the outcome?) _____

   g. discussed politics with you _____

   h. discussed politics positively and with hope _____

9. a. Which undergraduate college did you attend? _____

   b. Which law school did you attend? _____

   c. What was your academic rank in your law school class?

      top 1/3 _____

      middle 1/3 _____

      lower 1/3 _____

   d. How influential was law school on your thinking and subsequent career?

      very important _____

      moderately important _____

      not important _____

      If very important, tell how and why. _____

10. What was your first job after you graduated from law school? _____

    What was your primary *career* job before coming on the bench? _____

    What was your last job before coming on the bench? _____

11. How would you characterize your law practice? (check the appropriate box)

    solo practitioner _____

    urban _____

    criminal _____

    plaintiff _____

    mostly white _____

    trial _____

    with firm _____

    rural _____

    civil _____

    defendant _____

    mostly black _____

    nontrial _____

12. Which term best describes your political ideology before you went on the bench?

    liberal _____

    moderate _____

    conservative _____

    other _____

13. What was/is your political party affiliation?

    Democrat _____

    Republican _____

    Other _____

14. How active were you in party affairs before your appointment to the bench? (check where applicable)

    voter _____

    party member _____

    campaign worker _____

    party official _____

    campaign manager _____

    political advisor _____

    party contributor _____

    candidate _____

15. Tell me how you first became interested in politics?

    Primary Influence

    a. family _____

    b. friend _____

   c. teacher _____

   d. civil rights issues _____

   e. other (please name) _____

When

   a. youth _____

   b. adolescence _____

   c. college _____

   d. law school _____

   e. in law practice _____

   f. other _____

16. How did you first become *active* in politics?

   a. through political party _____

   b. through labor union _____

   c. in the civil rights movement _____

   f. through a friend _____

   e. other (please name) _____

17. How active were you in the civil rights movement?

very active _____

moderately active _____

not active _____

18. If active, which civil rights organization(s) were you active in or with?

NAACP _____

SCLC _____

Urban League _____

CORE _____

SNCC _____

Other (please name) _____

19. In   civil   rights   organization(s),   were   you

a member _____

a worker _____

a contributor _____

an officer _____

20. How did you first become interested in becoming a lawyer?

Primary Influence

   a. family _____

   b. friend _____

c. teacher _____

d. other (please name) _____

When

a. youth _____

b. adolescence _____

c. college _____

d. other _____

21. How did you first become interested in serving as a judge?

Primary Influence

a. family _____

b. friend _____

c. teacher _____

d. through law practice _____

e. other (please name) _____

When

a. youth _____

b. adolescence _____

c. college _____

d. law school _____

e. as lawyer _____

22. How did you go about becoming a judge after you first became interested? What did you do? Who did you see?

_____

_____

_____

_____

23. Some facts about your judicial position

a. Is your present court position at the trial level _____

appellate level _____

b. Is your court a single-membered one _____

multi-membered one _____

c. Is your judgeship an appointive one _____

elective one _____

partisan _____

nonpartisan _____

Missouri Plan _____

d. Were you initially appointed _____ to your present position?

elected _____ to your present position?

24. What do you think were the most important factors in your election or appointment to your judicial position?

   a. political party _____

   b. professional standing _____

   c. civil rights groups _____

   d. friends _____

   e. black voters _____

   f. press _____

   g. other (please name) _____

25. Do you think your race was an important help in your getting on the bench?

   Yes _____ No _____

26. The visibility of judgeships

   Are judgeships important instruments for realizing black equality and progress?

   Yes _____ No _____

   Do you think that black political leaders are sufficiently aware of the importance of judgeships as instruments for realizing black equality and progress?

   Yes _____ No _____

   Do you think that the average black person is sufficiently aware of the importance of judgeships as instruments for realizing black equality and progress?

   Yes _____ No _____

   Did black interest groups help you get your judgeships?

   Yes _____ No _____

   Should black interest groups help blacks get judgeships?

   Yes _____ No

27. Some people have said that ethnic group representatives, including judges, have come to their positions with the intention of protecting the interests of their ethnic group.

   Do black judges exercise their powers with a special view toward protecting the rights of blacks?

   Yes _____   No _____   Don't Know _____

Should they exercise their powers with a special view toward protecting the rights of blacks?

Yes _____ No _____ Don't Know _____

Do you exercise your powers with a special view toward protecting the rights of blacks?

Yes _____ No _____ Don't Know _____

Are courts political?

Yes _____ No _____ Don't Know _____

28. How would you characterize your judicial beliefs?

    a. liberal _____

    b. moderate _____

    c. conservative _____

    d. other _____

29. Do you primarily consider yourself to be a black judge? _____

    Or a judge who is black? _____

    Why? _____

30. As a judge, have you been discriminated against by

    a. white political leaders _____

    b. the police _____

    c. the press and media _____

    d. members of the bar _____

    e. your fellow judges _____

    f. other (please name) _____

    What form has this discrimination taken? _____

31. How pervasive is racism in the courts of your communtiy?

    a. high _____

    b. moderate _____

    c. low _____

32. Many studies have shown that blacks and the poor receive higher sentences than whites and the affluent who commit the same crime.

Do you think that black litigants are treated fairly in the courts of your community?

Yes _____ No _____ Don't Know _____

Do you find racially inequitable sentences on your court level?

Yes _____   No _____   Don't Know _____

Do you think that poor litigants are treated fairly in the courts of your community?

Yes _____   No _____   Don't Know _____

Do you find inequitable sentences between the poor and the affluent on your court level?

Yes _____   No _____   Don't Know _____

Do you consider jails as they exist today to be more for punishment than for rehabilitation?

Yes _____   No _____   Don't Know _____

Should jails be more for punishment than for rehabilitation?

Yes _____   No _____   Don't Know _____

33. Check the appropriate box.

How much racial progress has this country made in the last 20 years?

Very Much_____   Some_____   None_____

How much further does this country have to go to achieve racial equality?

Very Much_____   Some_____   None_____

How much have trial courts contributed to the achievement of racial progress?

Very Much_____   Some_____   None_____

How much *should* trial courts contribute to the achievement of racial progress?

Very Much_____   Some_____   None_____

34. Some people think that judges should be legal innovators, while others argue that judges should merely apply the law, leaving innovation to the legislatures. How do you feel about this?

   a. apply the law _____
   b. in-between _____
   c. innovate _____
   d. other (please name) _____

      Comment if you wish.

What percentage of the cases that come before you offer any real opportunity to innovate? _____

35. Judges and policymaking

To what extent do trial courts in your city make public policy?

Substantial_____ Some_____ None_____

To what extent do the judges on your court level attempt to make public policy?

Substantial_____ Some_____ None_____

To what extent do you attempt to make public policy?

Substantial_____ Some_____ None_____

To what extent should judges make public policy?

Substantial_____ Some_____ None_____

36. What difference does it make to the black community that you, a black person, are sitting as a judge? Why?

What difference does it make to the community at large?

37. What are the most important things you should do in your position as judge?

38. What is the hardest part of your job?

What is the best part of your job?

**If you wish to receive the results of this study, please indicate by checking the slot. _____

Bibliography

A decade and a half of inflation has turned seeming necessities into luxuries, for example, the underestimated and taken-for-granted footnote. In an effort to shave expenses, no footnotes appear in this book. However, to make life easy for readers, especially serious ones, information ordinarily contained in those citations has in many cases been transferred to the bibliography. Facts, assertions, beliefs, and theories, are placed with as much precision as possible within the bibliographic entries.

This new method of citation will of course demand extra exertion by the reader. In some instances, the name of the cited author appears in the text and the reader need only search alphabetically for the name. Yet, for reasons of style and flow of writing (and reading), this could not always be done. At such points, the reader must read through the section to find the source for which he is searching.

For the reader who wishes to read the original citation, be advised to scan the table of contents as well as the index to ease the difficulty of the search.

I hope this method of proceeding will cushion the disappointment of the reader, as we all seek new life-styles (and publishing formats) to assimilate the habits of the past into hospitable ones of the future.

Adamany, David. "The Party Variable in Judges' Voting: Conceptual Notes and a Case Study." *American Political Science Review* 62 (1962): 57-72. Finds that political party is related to judicial decisions at the state level.

———, and DuBois, Philip. "Electing State Judges." *Wisconsin Law Review.* vol. 1976, no. 3 (1976): 731-779. Compare judicial elections in the early and mid-1960s in Wisconsin to presidential and gubernatorial elections, looking at voter turnout. Conclude that election scheduling and ballot form "plainly" influence voter participation.

Adelson, Joseph, and O'Neil, Robert. "Growth of Political Ideas in Adolescence: The Sense of Community." *Journal of Personality and Social Psychology* 4 (1966): 295-306. Development of ideology depends on intellectual maturity.

Atkins, Burton M. "Judicial Elections." *Florida Bar Journal* vol. L, no. 3 (March

1976): 152-157. Provoked by perennial state legislative question of judicial selection, Burton canvases state bench to ascertain actual method of selection.

Barber, James A. *Social Mobility and Voting Behavior.* Chicago: Rand McNally and Company, 1970. Movement of individuals between classes, upward and downward, helps moderate political system.

Bartlett, Donald L., and Steele, James B. "Crime and Injustice." *Philadelphia Inquirer.* Week of 18 February 1973. This series of articles, based upon Philadelphia's criminal court computers, provide an invaluable and provocative journalistic account of arrests, trials, convictions, sentences, judges, and races.

Bell, D.A., Jr. "Racism in American Courts: Cause for Black Disruption or Despair?" *California Law Review* 61 (January 1973): 165. Race bias is present in civil as well as criminal courts.

Beveridge, Albert J. *The Life of John Marshall.* 4 vol. Boston: Houghton Mifflin Company, 1919. This pioneering example of the judicial biography seeks to tie attitudes to actions.

Biddle, Bruce J., and Thomas, Edwin J. *Role Theory: Its Concepts and Research.* New York: John Wiley and Sons, Inc., 1966. See especially ch. 1 for clarification of the components of role theory.

Billingsley, Andrew. *Black Families in White America.* Englewood Cliffs, N.J.: Prentice-Hall, Inc., 1968. A black sociologist challenges and clarifies white assessments of the condition of the black family.

Bowen, Don A. "The Explanation of Judicial Voting Behavior from Sociological Characteristics of Judges." Ph.D. dissertation, Yale University, 1965. Party, region, religion, income, tenure, and age, especially in aggregate, can explain selected decisions of state and federal courts.

Bowers, William L., and Pierce, Glenn L. "Arbitrariness and Discrimination under Post-Furman Capital Studies." *Crime and Delinquency.* vol. 26, no. 4 (October 1980): 563-641. Capital punishment cases in Ohio, Texas, Florida, and Georgia, are examined in the aftermath of state legislation that had been reworked to conform to United States Supreme Court *Furman* decision.

Brown, Lee. "The Victimizers." *Nation's Cities.* vol. 16, no. 9 (September 1978): 16-18. Federal and state prison and jail populations are listed by race from 1969 to 1976.

Brown v. Board of Education, 347 United States Reports 483 (1954). This case effectively outlawed all legal forms of racial segregation in public facilities.

Bullock, Henry Allen. "Significance of the Racial Factor in the Length of Prison Sentence." *Journal of Criminal Law, Criminology and Police Science* 52 (1961): 411-17. Race is an important factor in sentencing.

Burnham, David. "3 of 5 Slain by Police Here Are Black, Same as Rate of Arrest." *New York Times.* 26 August 1973, section 1, p. 1. Blacks are disproportionately represented in New York City Police slay and arrest records.

Burns, Hayward. "Can a Black Man Get a Fair Trial in This Country?" *New York Times Magazine.* 12 July 1970, cited in Gilbert Ware, ed. *From the Black Bar: Voices for Equal Justice* (see Ware entry). See p. 82 for listing of racial composition of executions in the United States 1930-66.

Campbell, Angus. *White Attitudes Toward Black People.* Ann Arbor, Michigan: Institute of Social Research, 1971. See p. 19 for discussion of variety of racial attitudes of white people.

Canon, Bradley C. "Characteristics and Career Patterns of State Supreme Court Justices." *State Government* 45 (1972): 34-41. State high court jurists are similar to their federal cohorts—white, male, and upper-class.

Carmichael, Stokely, and Hamilton, Charles V. *Black Power: The Politics of Liberation in America.* New York: Vintage Books, 1967. A history and criticism of black politics as well as a prescription for black liberation.

Carter, Robert. "The Black Lawyer." *The Humanist* (September/October 1969): 12-16. A well-known civil rights lawyer reflects on the role of the black bar in the movement for race equality.

Clark, Kenneth. "The Civil Rights Movement: Momentum and Organization." *The Black Revolt,* edited by James Geshwender. Englewood Cliffs, N.J.: Prentice-Hall, Inc., 1971. Social science activist characterizes civil rights organizations.

Cole, Leonard A. *Blacks in Power: A Comparative Study of Black and White Elected Officials.* Princeton, N.J.: Princeton University Press, 1976. A study of local officials in several New Jersey cities, which among other things, finds that the blacks surveyed are more likely to be Democratic and liberal than the whites.

Conyers, James E., and Wallace, Walter L. *Black Elected Officials: A Study of Black Americans Holding Governmental Office.* New York: Russell Sage Foundation, 1976. Black and white politicos are compared by attitudes, offices, and regions.

Cook, Beverly Blair. "Black Representation in the Third Branch." *Black Law Journal* 1 (1972): 260-79. This is a pioneering and provocative analysis of the origins of black judges.

Crockett, George. "The Role of the Black Judge." *Journal of Public Law* 20 (1971): 398-401. An article advocating judicial activism for black judges.

Curran, Barbara A. "Lawyer Demographics." Preliminary report of a two-volume statistical study of the American legal profession. Presented at the American Bar Association Annual Meeting. New Orleans, August 8, 1981. Employment, age, and sex of lawyers as of April 1980.

Dauer, Manning J. "Multi-Member Districts in Dade County: Study of a Problem and a Delegation." *Journal of Politics* 28 (1961): 617. Institutional rules should be expected to shape role attitudes.

Davidson, Roger H. *The Role of the Congressman.* New York: Pegasus Books, 1969. Congressmen are torn between getting reelected and becoming a congressional power.

Department of Commerce. Social Indicators III: Selected Data on Social Conditions and Trends in the United States. Washington, D.C.: Department of Commerce, Bureau of Census, December 1980. Government data provide insights on American race issues.

————. State and Metropolitan Area Data Book 1979: A Statistical Abstract Supplement. Washington, D.C.: Department of Commerce, Bureau of Census, 1980. A variety of economic and demographic information is presented.

Department of Labor: Handbook of Labor Statistics 1978. Washington, D.C.: Department of Labor, Bureau of Labor Statistics, June 1979. Positions of blacks and whites in American economy are compared.

Dexter, Lewis. *Elite and Specialized Interviewing.* Evanston, Illinois: Northwestern University Press, 1970. This small book provides guidelines and rationales for interviewing.

Dolbeare, Kenneth M. "The Federal District Courts and urban Public Policy: An Exploratory Study (1960-67)." In *Frontiers of Judicial Research,* edited by Joel Grossman and Joseph Tanenhaus. New York: John Wiley and Sons, Inc., 1969. 373-404. Federal trial courts are not intimate participants in local policy-making process.

Dred Scott v. Sanford, 19 Howard (United States Reports) 393 (1857). This is the infamous case in which U.S. Supreme Court Chief Justice Roger Taney said that black slaves had no rights and were still property no matter how long they had resided in a free state or territory.

DuBois, P.L. "Voter Turnout in State Judicial Elections: An Analysis of the Tail on the Electoral Kite." *Journal of Politics* 41 (August 1979): 865-88. Voter response to judicial elections is related to a host of institutional factors.

DuBois, W.E. Burghardt. *The Souls of Black Folk.* New York: Fawcett World Library, 1961. See p. 17 for comment on dual personality.

Easton, David, and Dennis, Jack. *Children in the Political System: Origins of Political Legitimacy.* New York: McGraw-Hill Book Company, 1969. An examination of the factors that influence the political socialization of children.

Edwards, G. Franklin. *The Negro Professional Class.* Glencoe, Illinois: Free Press, 1959. This study of black professionals is very useful since it follows Frazier's examination of black lawyers by a quarter-century.

Eulau, Heinz, and Sprague, John. *Lawyers in Politics.* Indianapolis: The Bobbs-Merrill Co., Inc., 1964. Law and politics are convergent since skills in former are useful in latter.

Gaudet, Frederick J. "Individual Differences in the Sentencing Tendencies of Judges." *Archives of Psychology* 22 (1938). Race is a factor in sentencing.

Gellhorn, Ernest. "The Law Schools and the Negro." *Duke Law Journal* (1968): 1069-99. Blacks are underrepresented in American law schools.

Glenn, Norval. "Aging and Conservatism." *The Annals of American Academy of Political and Social Science* 392 (September 1974): 176-186. Varying definitions of aging and conservatism are discussed.

Glick, Henry R. *Supreme Courts in State Politics: An Investigation of the Judicial Role.* New York: Basic Books, Inc., Publishers, 1971. Four state supreme courts are focus of role study.

Gockel, Garlen. "Income and Religious Affiliation: A Regression Analysis." *American Journal of Sociology* 74 (1969): 632-47. An analysis of why income is related to religious affiliation.

Goldman, Marian S. *A Portrait of the Black Attorney in Chicago.* Chicago: American Bar Foundation, 1972. Local study of black lawyers is useful for comparison to black lawyers nation-wide.

Goldman, Sheldon. "Politics, Judges, and the Administration of Justice: The Backgrounds, Recruitment, and Decisional Tendencies of Judges of the United States Courts of Appeals, 1961-64." Ph.D. dissertation, Harvard University, 1965. Provides the basis for his article, "Voting Behavior on the United States Courts of Appeals, 1961-64." *American Political Science Review* 60 (1966): 375-86; and the provocation for his article, "Voting Behavior on the United States Courts of Appeals Revisited." *American Political Science Review* 69 (1975): 491-506. All three are useful in comparing the social backgrounds, especially age, of federal appellate judges to the Afro-American bench. For political party as a factor in judicial appointments see his article, "Characteristics of Eisenhower and Kennedy Appointees to Lower Federal Courts." *Western Political Quarterly* 17 (1965): 755-62.

Goldstein, Tom. "City Hall Pickets Back Judge Wright." *New York Times.* 31 January 1974, p. 23. In addtion, a series of other articles on the Wright controversy, include Goldstein, "Wright to Go to Civil Court in Transfer of Nine Judges." *New York Times.* 17 December 1974, p. 41; "Bar Unit to Study Shift of a Judge." *New York Times.* 21 December 1974, p. 34; "Justice and Amount of Bail." *New York Times.* 22 December 1974, section 4, p. 5; and "Judge Wright, Focus of Dispute, Reassigned to Criminal Court." *New York Times.* 28 February 1978, p. 37.

Greer, Edward. "The Class Nature of Urban Police During the Period of Black Municipal Power." *Crime and Social Justice* 9 (Spring/Summer 1978): 54. Article examines how policymakers in police departments have remained heavily white as blacks gained electoral offices.

Gross, Neal; Mason, Ward S.; and McEachern, Alexander. *Explorations in Role Analysis: Studies of the School Superintendency Role.* New York: John Wiley and Sons, Inc., 1958. This seminal work span a host of role analysts. See p. 12 for distinctions and definitions of role.

Grossman, Joel. *Lawyers and Judges: The ABA and the Politics of Judicial Selection.* New York: Random House, Inc., 1964. Analysis of the influence of the organized bar on federal judicial appointments. For an application of role, see his "Role Playing and the Analysis of Judicial Behavior: The case of Mr. Justice Frankfurter." *Journal of Public Law* 1 (1962): 285-309.

Hacker, Andrew. "The Elected and the Anointed: Two American Elites." *American Political Science Review* 55 (1961): 539-48. Finds overrepresentation of high-status religious denominations at the highest levels of public and private sectors.

Henderson, Bancroft, and Sinclair, T.C. *The Selection of Judges in Texas: An Exploratory Study.* Houston: Public Affairs Research Center, 1965. This small study of state and local judges has proved a boon for comparative judicial scholars. Among other things, they find that bar associations and political party are factors in judicial appointments; de facto appointment of elective judgeships; and the prosecutor's office as a stepping-stone to the bench.

Hepburn, John R. "Race and the Decision to Arrest: An Analysis of Warrants Issued." *Journal of Research in Crime and Delinquency* vol. 15, no. 1 (1978): 54-73. All 1974 adults arrests (28,235) in a large midwestern city are analyzed to assess relationship between race and subsequent issuance of warrants by district attorney. Controlling for offense, age, sex, and racial composition of neighborhood, nonwhites continue to have a larger proportion than whites of arrests that are not upheld by issuance of a warrant, indicating that arrest is used by police as a tool of race harassment.

Hess, Robert D., and Torney, Judith V. *The Development of Political Attitudes in Children.* Chicago: Aldine Publishing Company, 1967. Small study traces influences of various sources on politicial socialization of children.

Hindelang, Michael J.; Gottfriend, Michael R.; and Flanagan, Timothy J., eds. *Sourcebook of Criminal Justice Statistics—1980.* U.S. Department of Justice, Bureau of Labor Statistics. Washington, D.C.: U.S. Government Printing Office, 1981. This compilation of numbers and tables documents progressively greater black presence as criminal enforcement system moves from arrest to imprisonment.

Hirsch, Herbert. *Poverty and Politicization in an American Subculture.* New York: The Free Press, 1971. Among other things, discusses apathy and alienation among America's poor people.

Holland, John L. *Making Vocational Choice: A Theory of Careers.* Englewood Cliffs, N.Y.: Prentice-Hall, Inc., 1973. A provocative book that relates vocational choice to personality. For attributes of legal personality, see pp. 15-17, 111.

Howard, J. Woodford. "Judicial Biography and the Behavioral Persuasion." *American Political Science Review* 65 (1971): 712. Discusses the merits and marriage of traditional biography to current behavioralism. For a particular example of this marriage, see his *Mr. Justice Murphy: A Political Biography*. Princeton, N.J.: Princeton University Press, 1968. See also his *Courts of Appeals in the Federal Judicial System: A Study of the Second, Fifth, and District of Columbia Circuits*. Princeton, N.J.: Princeton University Press, 1981. This last, with its aggregate data and conclusions on background and selection, is especially useful for comparison with black judges.

Huitt, Ralph. "The Morse Committee Assignment Controversy: A Study in Senate Norms." *American Political Science Review* 51 (1957): 313. See also his "The Outsider in the Senate: An Alternative Role." *American Political Science Review* 55 (1961): 566. These articles highlight the expectations and sanctions of role theory in real life setting.

Ish, Joel S. "Trial Judges in Urban Politics: A Comparative Analysis." Ph.D. dissertation, Johns Hopkins University, 1975. Study of trial judges in two cities and their suburban counties, which finds among other things, that office of prosecutor is major source for judge and that elective benches have become in fact appointive ones.

Jacob, Herbert. "The Effect of Institutional Differences in the Recruitment Process: The Case of State Judges." *Journal of Public Law* 13 (1964): 104-19. Finds no appreciable differences among appointive and elective judges.

Jacobs, James B., and Cohen, Jay. "The Impact of Racial Integration on Police." *Journal of Police Science and Administration* vol. 6, no. 2 (June 1978): 168-83. Racial integration of police forces has been slow.

———, and Kraft, Lawrence. "Integrating the Keepers: A Comparison of Black and White Prison Guards in Illinois." *Social Problems* 25 (February 1978): 304-18. No *consistent* differences found between these two groups.

Jaros, Dean. *Socialization to Politics*. New York: Praeger Publishers, Inc., 1973. Argues that socialization is a continuing process. See pp. 7-26 for analysis of transmission of religious faith from parents to children, and also of political values.

Jencks, Christopher, and Reisman, David. "The American Negro College." *Harvard Educational Review* 37 (1967): 3-60. Their conclusion that black colleges were "academic deserts" provoked a maelstrom of criticism and rebuttal.

Jennings, M. Kent, and Niemi, Richard C. "The Transmission of Political Values from Parent to Child." *American Political Science Review* 62 (1968): 169-84. Family transmits few political values beyond political party affiliation.

Johnson, Robert C. "Affirmative Action and the Academic Professions." *The Annals of the American Academy of Political and Social Sciences* vol. 448 (March 1980): 102-14. Pool of black academicians is small.

Johnston, Ruby F. *The Religion of Negro Protestants.* New York: Philosophical Library, 1956. Blacks are concentrated in Baptist and Methodist denominations.

Joint Center for Political Studies. National Roster of Black Elected Officials. Washington: Joint Center for Political Studies, vol. 10, 1981. Black elected officials are listed by office and state.

Jones, Mark E. "Racism in Special Courts." In *From the Black Bar Voices for Equal Justice,* edited by Gilbert Ware. (see Ware entry). See pp. 53-60 for discussion of racism in noncriminal courts.

Judicature Staff. "The Black Judge in America." *Judicature* 57 (June/July 1973): 18-25. Black bench is surveyed for demographic information.

Killen, John Oliver. *Black Man's Burden.* New York: Trident Press, 1965. An exposition of the effects that white racism has had upon blacks, especially upon their desire for change (see p. 21).

Knoke, David. "Religion, Stratification and Politics: America in the 1960s." *American Journal of Political Science* 18 (1974): 331-45. Class and religious affiliation are examined.

Knowles, Louis L., and Prewitt, Kenneth, eds. *Institutional Racism in America.* Englewood Cliffs, N.J.: Prentice-Hall, Inc., 1969. A provocative set of essays that details the ways in which "neutral" procedures put blacks and minorities at a disadvantage. One of its regretable effects was to remove the individual decision-maker from the context of policymaking.

Ladd, Everett Carll, ed. "Opinion Roundup: Minorities in the '70's." *Public Opinion* vol 3, no. 1 (December/January 1980): 37-38. In addition, see his "Opinion Roundup: The State of Race Relations—19081." *Public Opinion* vol. 4, no. 2 (April/May 1981): 32-40. Both articles provide samples of public opinion on race questions, quite often comparing black and white attitudes.

Landinsky, Jack. "The Impact of Social Backgrounds of Lawyers on Law Practice and the Law." *Journal of Legal Education* 16 (1963): 127-44. See his characterization of ethnic solo practtioners who are in many ways comparable to black practitioners.

Laue, James. "The Changing Character of Negro Protest." *The Annals of the American Academy of Political and Social Science* 357 (January 1965): 121. Provides a comparative assessment of the goals, assumptions, and tactics of the then-existing major civil rights groups.

Lazerwitz, Bernard. "A Comparison of Major United States Religious Groups." *Journal of American Statistical Association* 56 (1961): 568-79. Religious groups are ranked by education, occupation, and income.

Levin, Martin. "Urban Politics and Judicial Behavior." *Journal of Legal Studies* 1 (1972): 193-221. Examines the question of elective versus appointive benches by studying the behavior of the elective partisan courts in Pittsburgh and comparable appointive ones in Minneapolis.

Levitan, Sar A.; Johnston, William B.; and Taggart, Robert. *Still a Dream: The Chaning Status of Blacks Since 1960.* Cambridge, Mass.: Harvard University Press, 1975. A cornucopia of statistical information comparing the social conditions of blacks before and after the civil rights upheavals.

Lortie, Don R. "Professional Socialization." *Harvard Educational Review* 29 (1959): 363-s67. Law practice is more influential than law school on attitudes of lawyers.

Manderson, Marge. Affirmative Inaction: Public Employment in the Rural Black Belt. Atlanta: Southern Regional Council, 1980. A special report of approximately 25 pages focusing on racial discrimination in southern rural governments and compares 14 rural county and town payrolls in South Carolina, Georgia, and Alabama.

Mason, Gene. "Judges and Their Publics: Role Perceptions and Role Expectations." Ph.D. dissertation, University of Kansas, 1967. Public and professional expectations of judicial behavior do not determine judicial decisions.

Matthews, Donald. *The Social Background of Political Decision-Makers.* New York: Random House, Inc., 1954. See also *U.S. Senators and their World.* New York: Vintage Books, 1960. See especially ch. 5 for discussion of religious affiliations of national political elites.

Meyer, Marshall. "Police Shooting at Minorities: The Case of Los Angeles." *The Annals of the American Academy of Political and Social Sciences* 452 (November 1980): 98-110. Finds blacks disproportionately among those arrested, shot at, shot, and killed by the Los Angeles police department in a four-year period, 1974-78.

Miller, Marc. "The Numbers Game." *Southern Exposure* vol. 6, no. 4 (Winter 1978): 25-29. Lists executions in the United States, especially the South, from the 1930s to the 1960s.

Mitchell, William C. "Occupational Role Strains: The American Elective Official." *Administrative Science Quarterly* 3 (1958): 210. Competition between conflicting role expectations in the ongoing battle to define role.

Moynihan, Daniel P. "The Tangle of Pathology." In *The Black Family,* edited by Robert Staples. Belmont, Calif.: Wadsworth Publishing Company, 1971. Controversial government working paper seen by its many critics as blaming blacks for the deterioration of family structures.

Nachman, Barbara. "Childhood Experiences and Vocational Choice in Law, Dentistry, and Social Work." *Journal of Counseling Psychology* 7 (1960): 243-50. An early exposition that vocation is an expression of personality.

Nagel, Stuart. "Political Party Affiliation and Justices' Decisions." *American Political Science Review* 45 (1961): 843-51. Also see his "Ethnic Affiliation and Judicial Propensities." *Journal of Politics* 24 (1962): 92-110. Latter article finds association between religious denomination and judicial behavior.

Nie, Norman H.; Hull, C. Hadlai; Jenkins, Jean G.; Steinbrenner, Karin; and
Bent, Dale H. *Statistical Package for the Social Sciences,* 2d. rev. ed. New
York: McGraw-Hill Book Company, 1975. See pp. 222-228 for methodo-
logical discussion.

————; Verba, Sidney; and Petrocik, John R. *The Changing American Voter.*
Cambridge, Mass.: Harvard University Press, 1976. Black political party
alignment is discussed on p. 227; youth and liberalism on p. 264; and see ch.
13 for characterization of political party followers.

Oelsner, Leslie. "Wide Disparities Mark Sentencing Here." *New York Times.* 27
September 1972. Blacks are disproportionately represented in New York
City sentencing study.

Palmer, Dewey H. "Moving North: Migration of Negroes During World War
II." *Phylon* 28 (1967): 52-62. Discusses the push of the South and the pull of
the North as well as the lines of migration.

Parker, Seymour, and Kleiner, Robert. "Status Position, Mobility, and Ethnic
Identifcation of the Negro." *Journal of Social Issues* 20 (1964): 85-102.
Concludes that upwardly mobile blacks do not identify as closely with
blacks as a group as the downwardly mobile ones.

Patterson, Samuel C. "The Role of the Deviant in the State Legislative System:
The Wisconsin Assembly." *Western Political Quarterly* 14 (1961): 460.
Role theory is applicable to state legislatures.

Perry, Robert T. *Black Legislators.* San Francisco: R and E Associates, 1976. Ai
study of blacks in the Missouri legislature; their backgrounds and powers
are compared to their white fellows.

Plessy v. Ferguson, 163 United States Reports 537 (1896). This is the best-known
case in which the U.S. Supreme Court legitimated the doctrine of "separate
but equal" public facilities for blacks and whites.

Poole, Eric D., and Regoli, Robert M. "Race, Institutional Rulebreaking, and
Disciplinary Response: A Study of Discretionary Decision-Making in
Prison." *Law and Society Review* vol. 14, no. 4 (Summer 1980): 931-46. A
study of guard response to infractions of prisoners in a medium-security
prison for adult male felons, with finding that while black and white
rulebreaking was equally likely, blacks were more likely to be officially
reported for infractions.

Prewitt, Kenneth. *The Recruitment of Political Leaders: A Study of Citizen-
Politicians.* Indianapolis: The Bobbs-Merrill Co., Inc., 1970. A study of
city councilmen in the California Bay area. See p. 66 for estimate of
parental influence on political activists.

Pope, Carl E. "Postarrest Release Decisions: An Empirical Examination of
Social and Legal Criteria." *Journal of Research in Crime and Delinquency*
vol. 15, no. 1 (January 1978): 35-53. An examination of influences of social
and legal criteria in postarrest decisions to release 1,196 burglary arrestees
prior to trial in six California jurisdictions during a one-year period, ending

May 1973. Finds that blacks are disproportionately denied pretrial release.

Pritchett, C. Herman. *The Roosevelt Court: A Study in Judicial Politics and Values 1937-47.* New York: Macmillan Publishing Co., Inc., 1949. A path-breaking study of aggregate voting behavior of the U.S. Supreme Court justices and the deduction of attitudes from acts.

Report of National Advisory Commission on Civil Disorders. New York: Bantam Books, 1968. United States is becoming two societies—white and black.

Rich, Francis M., Jr. "Role Perception and Precedent Orientation as Variables Influencing Appellate Judicial Decision-Making: An Analysis of the Fifth Circuit Court of Appeals." Ph.D. dissertation, University of Georgia, 1967. Role attitudes affect judicial decisions.

Ridenhour, Ron. "Breaking the Code." *Figaro* vol. 10, no. 29 (July 20, 1981): 1, 5-6. A report of how a black former policeman successfully sued the New Orleans police department after refusing to sign a statement covering for his partner, also black.

Rose, Winfield, and Chia, Tiang Ping. "The Impact of Equal Employment Opportunity Act of 1972 on Black Employment in Federal Service: A Preliminary Analysis." *Public Administration Review* vol. 38, no. 3 (May/ June 1978): 245-51. Study of the General Schedule and other pay schedules and concludes that blacks in upper federal salary levels had not been increased as of May 1974.

Rosenblum, Victor G. *Law as a Political Instrument.* New York: Random House, Inc., 1961. Politics pervades legal system in diverse ways.

Sayre, Wallace S., and Kaufman, Herbert. *Governing New York City: Politics in the Metropolis.* New York: Russell Sage Foundation, 1960. A detailed look at Gotham politics, with a small section on judiciary.

Schmidhauser, John R. "The Justices of the Supreme Court: A Collective Portrait." *Midwest Journal of Political Science* 3 (1959): 1-57. Supreme Court jurists are from social-legal elites.

Schubert, Glendon. "Behavioral Jurisprudence." *Law and Society Reivew* 2 (1968): 407-28. Argues that beliefs may be deduced from bench actions. See his book, *The Constitutional Polity.* Boston: Boston University Press, 1970. See p. 118-29 for discussion of the relationship of aging and judging.

Schuman, Howard. "Attitudes vs. Actions Versus Attitudes vs. Attitudes." *Public Opinion Quarterly* 36 (1972): 347-54. Posits the argument that attitude is a limited factor in the actions of individuals and concludes that attitudes do influence behavior under certain circumstances.

————, and Hatchett, Shirley. *Black Racial Attitudes: Trends and Complexities.* Ann Arbor, Mich.: Institute for Social Research, 1974. Examines outlook of blacks in Detroit in the aftermath of the 1967 riot. Definitely for the specialist or serious student of interviewing techniques. However, see p. 56-73 for dissection of sources and degrees of political alienation.

Schuman, Jerome. "A Black Lawyer's Study." *Howard Law Journal* 16 (Winter 1971): 225. Looks at the socioeconomic backgrounds and careers of black bench and bar.

Secord, Paul F., and Backman, Carl W. *Social Psychology.* New York: McGraw-Hill Book Company, 1974. Ch. 10 and 11 provide much of the basis for our discussion of role.

Sellin, Thorstein. "Race Prejudice in the Administration of Justice." *American Journal of Sociology* 41 (1935). Pioneering study documents race disparities in capital cases.

Selltiz, Claire; Wrightsman, Lawrence S.; and Cook, Stuart W. *Research Methods in Social Relations.* New York: Holt, Rinehart and Winston, 1976. Mailed surveys and personal interviews are urged, since the complement each other.

Smith, D. Alton. "Government Employment and Black/White Relative Wages." *Journal of Human Resources* XV (Winter 1980): 87-98. Notes that blacks are noticeable for their prevalence at the lower end of the government pay scale; ascribes pattern to lack of promotions.

Southern Regional Council. *Race Makes a Difference: An Analysis of Sentence Disparities Among Black and White Offenders in Southern Prisons.* Atlanta: Southern Regional Council, 1969. Finds that blacks in state prisons were sentenced to longer terms than whites.

Spaeth, Harold. "An Approach to the Study of Attitudinal Differences as an Aspect of Judicial Behavior." *Midwest Journal of Political Science* 5 (1961): 165-80. The attitudes of Justices Black and Douglas influenced their voting behavior.

Stinner, William F., and DeJong, Gordon F. "Southern Negro Migration: Social and Economic Components of an Ecological Model." *Demography* 6 (1969): 455-71. Age, economics, geography, and culture both pushed and pulled blacks from the South.

Stone, Pauline T. "Social Bias in the Recruitment of Black Elected Officials in the United States." *Review of Black Political Economy* 8 (Summer 1978): 384-404. A Study of the socioeconomic backgrounds of state and local, elective and appointive officials in the state of Michigan.

Styles, Fitzhugh Lee. *The Negro Lawyers' Contribution to 71 Years of our Progress.* Philadelphia: Summer Press, 1934. Black bar has long been active in fight for race equality.

Taeuber, Karl E., and Taeuber, Alma F. "Changing Character of Negro Migration." *American Journal of Sociology* 70 (1965): 429-41. Discusses the socioeconomic character of blacks out of the South in the post-World War II period and the pattern of the movement.

Uhlman, Thomas M. *Racial Justice: Black Judges and Defendants in an Urban Trial Court.* Boston: Lexington Books, 1979. Besides our own study, this is the only full-length examination of the black bench in the United States.

The results of its sophisticated methodological comparison of black and white judges on one specific tribunal will provide data by which we can gauge our own findings and conclusions.

Ulmer, Sidney. "The Longitudinal Behavior of Hugo Lafayette Black: Parabolic Support for Civil Liberties, 1937-1971." *Florida University Law Review* 1 (Winter 1973): 131-58. Discusses and discards the idea that Justice Black became more conservative with increasing age.

United States Constitution, Article I, section 2, paragraph 3. Description of black slaves as three fifths of a person for tax and representative purposes.

Vines, Kenneth N. "The Judicial Role in the American States: An Exploration." In *Frontiers of Judicial Research,* edited by Joel Grossman and Joseph Tanenhaus. New York: John Wiley and Sons, Inc., 1969. See p. 476 for finding that judicial recruitment method has an immaterial affect on ideology of judges. For the influence of race on white federal district court judges, see his article, "Federal District Judges and Race Relations Cases in the South." *Journal of Politics* 26 (1964): 337-57.

Wahlke, John C.; Eulau, Heinz; Buchanan, William; and Ferguson, Leroy. *The Legislative System: Explorations in Legislative Behavior.* New York: John Wiley and Sons, Inc., 1962. Early discussion and study of role theory.

Ware, Gilbert, ed. *From the Black Bar: Voices for Equal Justice.* New York: G.P. Putnam's Sons, Capricorn Books, 1976. A collection of provocative essays by and about the black bar and bench. Discusses among other things racism in the bar examinations, race of prosecutors in big cities, and racial makeup of American bench and bar. See especially the introductory essay.

Warren, Bruce. "Socio-economic Achievement and Religion: The American Case." *Sociological Inquiry* 40 (1970): 130-55. Religious membership is related to socio-economic mobility.

Watson, Richard, and Downing, Rondal G. *The Politics of the Bench and the Bar: Judicial Selection Under the Missouri Nonpartisan Court Plan.* New York: John Wiley and Sons, inc., 1969. The examination of the compromise solution to the perennial problem of selection method for judges—election or appointment. Notes party and professional bar as factors in recruitment.

Weinstein, Alan G. "Predicting Behavior from Attitudes." *Public Opinion Quarterly* 36 (1972): 355-60. Studies arguments that attitudes do not affect actions.

Weissberg, Robert. *Political Learning, Political Choice, and Democratic Citizenship.* Englewood Cliffs, N.J.: Prentice-Hall, Inc., 1974. See pp. 13-14 for argument that religious denomination and political party identification are transmitted across generations.

Wilson, James Q. "Two Negro Politicians: An Interpretation." *Midwest Journal of Political Science* 4 (November 1960): 346-69. Compares the styles, careers, and electoral bases of Chicago Congressman William Dawson and New York Congressman Adam Clayton Powell. See also his book, *Negro Politics: The Search for Leadership.* New York: The Free Press, 1960.

Wold, John T. "Internal Procedures, Role Perceptions, and Judicial Behavior: A Study of Four State Courts of Last Resort." Ph.D. dissertation, Johns Hopkins University, 1972. See the derivative article, "Political Orientations, Social Backgrounds, and Role Perceptions of State Supreme Court Judges." *Western Political Quarterly* 27 (1975): 247. Finds among other things that judicial recruitment method does not affect ideological composition of bench.

Woodson, Carter G. *The Negro Professional Man and the Community: With Special Emphasis on the Physician and the Lawyer.* New York: Negro Universities Press, 1969. Provides a comparative benchmark of the black lawyer in the 1930s.

Wright, Bruce. "A Black Brood on Black Judges." *Judicature* 57 (June/July 1973): 22-23. Posits argument for maintaining elective benches in increasingly black jurisdictions.

Yinger, Milton J. *Toward a Field Theory of Behavior: Personality and Social Structure.* New York: McGraw-Hill Book Company, 1965. See pp. 99-101 for discussion of role theory.

Zisk, Betty; Eulau, Heinz; and Prewitt, Kenneth. "City Councilmen and the Group Struggle: A Typology of Role Orientations." *Journal of Politics* 27 (1965): 618. Also, see another of their articles on the role of California Bay area councilmen, "Political Socialization and Political Roles." *Public Opinion Quarterly* 30 (1966): 569.

Index